D1639453

Think Like a Vegan

Special thanks to **Super Thinkers**

Jane Patterson
Sebastiano Cossia Castiglioni
Roger Leese

Think Like a Vegan

What everyone can learn from vegan ethics

Emilia A. Leese and
Eva J. Charalambides

unbound

This edition first published in 2021

Unbound
TC Group, Level 1, Devonshire House,
One Mayfair Place, London W1J 8AJ

www.unbound.com

Text design by Ellipsis, Glasgow

A CIP record for this book is available from the British Library

ISBN 978-1-80018-018-5 (trade hbk)
ISBN 978-1-80018-019-2 (ebook)

Printed and bound by CPI Group (UK) Ltd, Croydon, CR0 4YY

1 3 5 7 9 8 6 4 2

Contents

If you have to compromise, be sure to compromise up.
Eleanor Roosevelt

To Roger

To Matt

Introduction

In this book, we ask you to set aside any preconceived notions about veganism and let yourself be open to our conversations. Through a personal, often imperfect and sometimes irreverent lens, we explore a variety of contemporary topics related to animal use and veganism in the context of everyday modern life. From the basics of vegan logic, to politics, economics, love and other aspects of being human, every chapter invites you into a thought-provoking conversation about your daily ethical decisions.

We present to you a series of essays for discussion, culminating in the final chapter, where we challenge you to apply the broad concepts explored throughout the book to practical thought experiments. In addition, at the end of each chapter, you will find *Takeaways* summarising the principal ideas we've covered in each. By combining exploratory essays alongside hypothetical scenarios, we aim to help readers accomplish two goals. First, to think about veganism as the simple concept that using animals is unjustified and unnecessary. And second, to encourage and facilitate positive and productive conversations within and across social communities.

We don't believe you need another source of heartrending pictures or descriptions of gore relating to animal farming attempting to guilt you into something. We offer an alternative by engaging you in conversations and giving you the tools to navigate the issues and arrive at your own conclusions. If, like us, you're concerned about animals, people, health and the environment, we aim to show you how all these concerns are connected and how veganism is the ethical choice addressing them. We'll do this by sharing personal stories about how we became vegan, exploring the basic ethical ideas underpinning veganism and by showing how half-measures, such as fur, cruelty or meat reduction campaigns, are ultimately unsatisfactory.

We want our essays to enable you to analyse and pull apart ethical issues, questions and dilemmas you might face related to using animals for food. These essays will act as benchmarks for your rediscovery of the ways by which you view the human use of animals.

From our own experiences, we know anyone can understand veganism and we can be especially effective in discussing it with others when we take the time to be informed and think with clarity. You may find some of our positions challenge a variety of socially accepted norms or practices: brilliant. We hope these challenges will help all of us question our choices and actions. After all, we should always be asking *why* we do what we do.

Although our primary focus in this work is the injustice of animal use, we recognise that society's *systemic* injustices are related and interconnected. Seeking a fair world for animals means we must also seek to reject and redress the injustices perpetrated on humans. These aren't mutually exclusive goals, or mutually exclusive ideas. Seeing the vulnerability of one will open our mind, eyes and heart to the other. All human injustices may be opposed, fought, addressed, dismantled, read, written, learned and talked about, whilst sticking to eating plants and being vegan.

If you're not vegan and, through this book, we provide you with compelling reasons for you to choose veganism, then great! If you're not yet ready to go vegan, we believe this book is still a valuable resource for everyone to make new, thoughtful connections with ethical principles in their lives.

For *how* to go vegan, there are many free and helpful resources online. Simple searches on the Internet, in your public library or local bookshop will yield many resources for vegan recipes and tips on cooking, where to find anything from vegan clothing, footwear and accessories, personal care and home cleaning products, to vegan restaurants in your city and elsewhere. For nutrition advice, we recommend consulting the resources we cite in Chapter 5 and the appropriate medical and nutritional professionals near you. And we're always happy to help with your questions. Contact us at ThinkLikeAVeganBook@gmail.com.

Emi & Eva

CHAPTER 1

Basics

What it means to be vegan and the basic ethical concepts at its heart.

What Does It Mean to Be Vegan?

In this first essay, we set out the fundamental concepts. From who vegans are, to the meaning of the terms *vegan* and *speciesism*, to the core problem of use, each of these concepts will echo throughout this book. We also reconcile the reality of being vegan in a non-vegan world, and recognise the interconnections of oppression with a call to reject all bigotry.

Vegans are just like you, we promise

Despite the stereotypes, you won't necessarily recognise a vegan. Vegans come in all ages, shapes, colours, sizes, religions, sexual orientations, gender identities, socio-economic backgrounds or classes, levels of education, senses of fashion, physical abilities, geographical locations, politics and any other differences in our human family. Very few people are vegan from birth. Most vegans have only been vegan for part of their lives. Some initially balked at the idea of veganism or rejected the concepts multiple times.

All vegans have one thing in common: a moment where a thought, a realisation or an argument for veganism resonated with them to such an extent they embraced changing their mind and behaviour about how they related to animals. That moment when something confronts us and challenges our usual way of thinking or of doing things, that's the crack in our understanding. That's the moment we let the light in to make change happen.[1]

Rejecting speciesism

Speciesism is the notion that humans are superior to animals. This notion is the current norm accepted by the overwhelming majority of people. Speciesism manifests itself in our viewing animals as objects and using them in a variety of ways, primarily for food.

Therefore, *to the extent possible and practicable*, vegans avoid using animals for food, clothing, entertainment or any other purpose. This means vegans don't consume animal flesh, fish, insects, molluscs, eggs, dairy, cheese and honey; don't ride horses, visit zoos or aquariums; and don't wear leather, fur, wool or silk.

Vegans reject speciesism and accept animals into the same moral sphere as humans with respect to fundamental rights, such as the right to live and the right to be free from ownership as another's property. The basis for this is the basic rule of fairness: accord the same moral treatment to everyone, unless there's a morally relevant reason to justify treating someone differently (for example, not allowing human children, or non-human animals, the vote).

How are non-human animals and human animals the same and why should we share the same moral sphere? We all belong to the animal kingdom, with humans evolving later than many non-human animal species. Put simply, all animals, including humans, aren't *objects*. We understand this when we look at our companion animals and it's not a new concept. Around 530 BCE, Pythagoras, Greek philosopher and mathematician, believed animals weren't objects based on his belief in the transmigration of souls.[2] Around 1190 CE, Maimonides, one of the most influential Jewish philosophers and scholars, wrote, 'It should not be believed that all beings exist for the sake of the existence of humanity. On the contrary, all the other beings too have been intended for their own sakes and not for the sake of something else.'[3] Maimonides recognised animals for themselves, not in relation to humans. He also wrote, 'Animals feel very great pain, there being no difference regarding this pain between humankind and the other animals. For the love and the tenderness of a mother for her child is not consequent upon reason, but upon the activity of the imaginative faculty, which is found in most animals just as it is found in humankind.'[4] British lawyer and philosopher Jeremy Bentham further advanced Western ethical notions of animals when, in the eighteenth century, he wrote:

'The day may come, when the rest of the animal creation may acquire those rights which never could have been withholden from them but by the hand of tyranny . . . What else is it that should trace the insuperable line? Is it the faculty of reason, or, perhaps, the faculty of discourse? But a full-grown horse or dog, is beyond comparison a more rational, as well as a more conversible animal than an infant of a day, or a week, or even a month old. But suppose the case were otherwise, what would it avail? the question is not, Can they *reason*? nor, Can they *talk*? but, Can they *suffer*?'[5]

Since then, many other philosophers and ethicists have continued to develop these notions (see Further Reading at the end of this book). This common thread of existence and experience between human animals and non-human animals is what sentience is all about; we're all sentient creatures. Sentience isn't whether one animal or another has imagination or is able to do some activity based on what people can do. To be universally meaningful, the recognition of sentience must be based on something broader. By sentience we mean simply having a desire to live, 'because sentience is a means to the end of continued existence',[6] as animal rights lawyer and philosopher Gary Francione explains; or as animal rights philosopher Tom Regan argues, 'We are each of us the experiencing subject of a life, a conscious creature having an individual welfare that has importance to us whatever our usefulness to others.'[7] And all animals demonstrate this desire to live in their own ways.

All animals have needs, wants, fears, abilities, intelligence, skills, social habits and emotions, which they demonstrate in ways like, and different from, humans. One animal may not be intelligent, whilst another may be more intelligent than a three-year-old human. One may be cute, the other less so. This doesn't mean these are morally relevant differences. These differences don't determine whether an animal should forfeit their life, just like they don't make similar determinations with respect to people. We don't need to research deeply to find stories of animal intelligence, social skills, emotional suffering or even empathy, whether farm animals or wild animals, such as whales, elephants or primates. We must apply the basic rule of fairness to animals because animals, like people, are sentient. Our shared sentience is the only morally relevant starting point from which to analyse whether the basic rule of fairness also applies to animals. Therefore, restating the basic rule of fairness to include animals: we owe animals the same moral treatment as people, unless there's a morally relevant reason to justify treating animals differently.

PLANT SENTIENCE

Plants aren't sentient. They are, of course, alive and complex. Unlike animals, they don't have a central nervous system. They *react* to stimuli, such as the sun, water and predators. Plants don't *respond* to stimuli. Sentient creatures *respond*: they run, cry out, fight, play, feel fear and pleasure, learn, use tools, dream.

We don't, or at least we can agree we shouldn't, deny humans fundamental rights if they have different needs, wants, fears, abilities, intelligence, skills, social habits or emotions.

Understanding we owe a group the same moral treatment is important because it makes clear these essential rights aren't something we give and take as we fancy or as a matter of our kindness. When it comes to non-human animals, we routinely ignore the basic rule of fairness and its principle of same moral treatment. We deny them the fundamental right to live. This is the current and normal reality everywhere and it has been so for at least 10,000 years, since we began animal husbandry.

Just because animal use is pervasive in our world doesn't mean it's our only choice. We have no morally relevant reason for treating animals differently when it comes to essential rights. The reasons we give for using animals are arbitrary and self-serving: we like eating, wearing and using them. We gain pleasure from using their products or their bodies, when we have *no need* to do so. Generally, we're also resistant to change, using history and tradition as excuses for a variety of behaviours, especially using animals. All our reasons are centred around human choices, ideas and desires, not on anything inherent in the animals themselves. In addition, our laws make it easy to continue using them because all animals, either explicitly or implicitly, are categorised as objects, or property, managed by either the state or their human *owners* to suit their needs and wants.

We can choose to see, address and dismantle human superiority. How? We can choose veganism.

DONALD WATSON'S DEFINITION

In 1944, Donald Watson and his future wife Dorothy Morgan coined the term vegan and its definition in response to the changing habits of vegetarians who were adding eggs and dairy back into their diets. Although it's a unique term, there were people living as vegans as part of their culture prior to Watson and Morgan coining the term. Veganism has never been an exclusively European or Western experience.[8]

Animals and ownership

Animals are owned, just like shoes, a laptop or phone. This comes as a surprise to many. It's the truth the world over. Broadly speaking, animals in the wild are the property of the state for the benefit of its people.[9] All other animals are the property of whoever bought them, be they individuals or companies. They are property just like your phone, a furnished house or the trees in a field you purchased. Their use and value are determined by their owner, regardless of the animal's own desires, wants and needs. By legally being entitled to view animals as physical property, an owner can use and dispose of animals at will, with little regard to the animal's basic rights to live free from exploitation. What's stark about this reality is the fact these basic rights to life and autonomy are seldom considered by their owners; they're never discussed and are rarely applied with respect to most animals.

To diminish our collective complicity in denying animals their basic, fundamental rights, and to maximise the economic value of animal bodies and products, we have developed legal frameworks setting minimum welfare or anti-cruelty standards.[10] These standards all assume using animals as objects is morally legitimate. These laws only work within the existing framework of animals as objects we own. What's more, these types of laws and standards only regulate how we use animals and, ultimately, how we're permitted to kill them. Other types of laws, such as anti-poaching or endangered species protection laws, only operate to protect specific species of animals simply because their extinction would damage a human interest. Whether the interest is fishing, tourism or national identity, the animal is protected for the benefit of people, not because the animals are entitled to an inherent right to live and not be an object. In the highest sense of irony, human activity has pushed these animals to such extreme conditions, threatening their survival, that we're now *protecting* species we've neglected, used and abused for our own benefit in the first place.

Objectification, both in law and in practice, makes it impossible to make any lasting transformative changes for the benefit of animals. For people, objectification in society affects us in a variety of ways and in numerous scenarios in our everyday lives. But we're not classified as objects under the law. This key difference enables recognition and protection of fundamental rights when it comes to humans, who are viewed as being individuals, versus how we consider our relationship with animals. It's impossible to either recognise or protect fundamental rights of an object because an object has no rights; it only has a purpose for its owner.

On an individual level, vegans' refusal to use animals as objects acknowledges their moral right to live free of exploitation. Any incremental change in laws affecting animals, although superficially beneficial, won't change the fact people use animals with abandon without, in great part, having morally relevant reasons to do so. Because of this, all the authors' work recognises the fundamental goal of abolishing the legal notion of animals as property.[11] Whether this is a goal we see materialise in our lifetime is immaterial; it's a goal worth thinking and talking about. After all, it was once considered unnatural for women to vote or have autonomy over their own lives.

Use is the problem

Imagine you contract an infection after swimming in a polluted river. You might visit a doctor and treat the symptoms. They'll disappear after treatment, until you swim in the river once again and become re-infected. The root of the problem is obviously the pollution in the river, only you decide to keep treating the symptoms each time they reoccur. Of course, treating the symptoms is a relevant and necessary exercise, but unless you address the root of the problem, treatment becomes part of a vicious circle.

We can analogise the river infection in the context of animals as objects for our use. Using animals is the root of the problem. A symptom of the problem is how animals are treated. Being concerned about how animals are treated before they become our food, clothing, furniture or whatever, is a relevant inquiry. It's like the recurring infection. The animals may be treated differently, but they'll continue to die. Just as with any disease, eradicating the fundamental problem itself must be the focus of any intervention. Hence why this book focuses on animal use as the problem.

No one wants to witness or know of animal mistreatment happening. In fact, it happens daily: all animals destined for human consumption end up dead, and none of them want to be dead. We can treat them as nicely as we want. In the end, they'll all die and become objects for us to use, eat or wear.

THE LUXURY HOTEL THOUGHT EXPERIMENT

You, your friends and family, including adults, newborns, toddlers, children and elders, live in a luxury hotel. All your needs are met. You sleep in the world's most comfortable bed and eat the best food. You have plenty of room and can roam around the premises and gardens as you please. Your every whim is satisfied. It sounds idyllic, doesn't it? However, none of you can leave the hotel. In fact, everyone's body provides one or more products that consumers want because they like them. Each night, someone comes along and kills or takes a friend or member of your family, including the babies and children, until it's your turn to die or be taken.

Of course, it's good to live in the lap of luxury, and less harm is much better than more harm. Still, you all die an unnatural death, whether quickly and painlessly or prolonged and terrifyingly. You're being protected from harm until the very worst harm is brought upon you: being killed. And for what reason? Because you're considered an object whose sole purpose in life is to provide an unnecessary product to those who wish to buy it, simply because they like it.

Some people object to this thought experiment because they say animals have no sense of time, they don't know what will happen to them, and they wouldn't be living in daily anguish like we would be. Maybe that's true. Even if they don't have a sense of time or know what will happen to them, does it really make a difference in deciding if it's right for us to use and kill them? And should it make a difference to us as the inflictors of this harm when we know exactly what will happen to them and we decide to do it anyway?

Let's examine these questions by going back to the basic rule of fairness and adding sentience as its basis: all sentient beings deserve and are entitled to the same treatment, unless there's a relevant moral difference.

THE UNCONSCIOUSNESS THOUGHT EXPERIMENT

Imagine someone who is unconscious. They're not brain dead; they're just in a very deep sleep from which they can't be awakened. Society steps in to safeguard that individual's interest in continued life because they can't do it themselves. In other words, the sleeper is sentient despite being unconscious. They too live and are treated well in the same luxury hotel your family, friends, children and yourself are living in. They're exploited for a specific bodily product. When their utility is spent, they're killed.

As people with a moral compass, we want the unconscious person to be treated well. We also wouldn't wish for them to be exploited or killed, despite being unable to consciously perceive what's happening to them. In the given scenario, the individual is treated as a thing, and we'd view this as morally reprehensible. We'd object because whether the unconscious individual has a sense of time or doesn't know what will happen to them wouldn't be relevant moral considerations determining whether they should be exploited and killed. In addition, we'd know what would be in store for them. The resulting harm, whether on them individually, their family or society at large, would be something we'd want to guard against.

The reasoning is the same with animals. Irrespective of whether they're perceived as having a higher level of consciousness, they're sentient and they'll all be killed one day. We use them as objects and we dispose of them as objects. When we take this into account and apply the analogous rationale, it's clear there's no morally relevant distinction between them and us. Sentience binds us together morally. Therefore, how can we begin to justify such radically different moral treatment between animals and humans?

A NOTE ON AGES OF FARM ANIMALS FOR

SLAUGHTER COMPARED TO NATURAL LIFESPAN

'The highest quality beef comes from animals that are under thirty-six months of age. Old cows produce highly acceptable beef if properly fattened and processed. Depending on the calf and the feeding regime, calves are best slaughtered between three and sixteen weeks of age. Hogs may be killed any time after they reach six weeks of age, but for the most profitable pork production they may need to be fed for five to ten months. Sheep and goats may be killed anytime after six weeks, but the more desirable age is from six to twelve months.'[12] According to a scientific study in the UK, slaughtering cows at twelve months is most profitable.[13]

Poultry is slaughtered between the ages of thirty-six and sixty days, depending on weight. Organic poultry is generally slaughtered at ninety-eight days.[14]

The natural lifespan of farm animals who don't end up slaughtered is between seven and twenty years.

Being vegan in a non-vegan world

We all live in a non-vegan world, so it's sometimes impossible or impracticable to completely avoid using animals. For example, some medicines, money, roads, equipment, computers and home and office insulation or building materials may contain animal ingredients. We may have to use one or all those things to carry on living a practical life in this world. Doing so doesn't mean one is no longer vegan. Just as a vegan is still a vegan if they were to purchase fruit and vegetables in a market from a non-vegan vendor or a non-vegan farmer, or if those fruit and vegetables were carried to market on a cart pulled by a horse or donkey.

An alternative way of explaining this conflict is thus: you're a committed pacifist. You also pay mandatory taxes to a government waging war. This doesn't make you a supporter of the war; rather, it just keeps you functioning in society so you can continue opposing war.

Humans are omnivores, meaning we can feed ourselves on either plants or animals. Whether other animals eat other animals is immaterial to human nutrition. We can't compare how we eat to how other animals eat because other animals have different nutritional needs than we do. If we compare ourselves to other primates, our closest biological relatives, we'll find they're primarily vegan. In addition, we have a choice of what we eat. We farm our food or go to shops and purchase foods farmed for us. Other primates don't have that choice or those cultural habits.

Rejecting all bigotry

In addition to rejecting speciesism, being vegan is a basic moral obligation akin to rejecting bigotry based on race, class, ethnicity, religion, country of origin, sexual orientation, sex and gender, physical and mental ability, appearance and age. Rejection of bigotry must be a component of veganism, and vice versa, precisely because of the equal treatment principle: it applies in all cases. If all sentient beings are morally equal, they deserve equal moral treatment. These are simple moral baselines, no more and no less.

This doesn't mean we won't find vegans who are bigoted or even speciesist. Just as we sometimes find sexism and misogyny among those who support women's issues and classism amongst those opposing racism. This view also doesn't equate human-animal suffering with non-human-animal suffering or minimise anyone's plight. Animals can't themselves explain to us why they deserve fundamental rights like humans, or go into detail about their suffering, needs, desires or abilities. We can only observe them and learn from their reactions what they might be experiencing, feeling or needing. What's clear is how we oppress them, just as we can see how we oppress other humans – oppression is oppression. Although we'd no longer skip consulting an oppressed or aggrieved group of people before addressing their oppression and grievances, when it comes to animals we must be more creative. Because they can't communicate these arguments to us in our language or using our ideas and symbols, some level of analogy is necessary to facilitate our reflection of others' suffering. We need to consider their suffering in relational terms to previous knowledge based on our beliefs. Through the lens of our own experiences, history, literature and philosophy, we learn how we should view the oppression of animals in a relatable and personal sense.

What Would Be the Answer in a Human Context?

Aren't animals different from humans? Yes, only in the sense each is a different species of animal from the other. *They* and *we* are all animal species. We've manufactured and developed the concept of species to make sense of the natural world and it's helpful in doing that. Species is only relevant in a scientific enquiry, not a moral one. So, whenever we find ourselves being asked about the human use of animals, or how to frame a response to an ethical question involving animals, we ask ourselves a simple question: what would be the thought process and answer if the question came up in a human context?

For example, whether we choose to wear leather, wool, silk or fur. What would be the answer in a human context? Would we knowingly wear the hair of a human who was forcibly shaved, whose sole purpose in living was to give us their hair? The answer would be no, obviously. Satisfying our vanity isn't a morally relevant reason to justify taking someone's hair without their permission. With humans who donate or sell their hair which are made into wigs or extensions, we assume consent, and even then, we're ready to scrutinise a process which is sometimes questionable in moral practice.[15] An animal can't ever give consent to give up their life, skin, hair or fur.

A trickier question is whether to support initiatives favouring reducing eating or harming animals. On the one hand, reducing harm is good, but when we support these initiatives who and what are we compromising, for whose benefit, and is it necessary to lend our support? When we support an *eat less meat* or an *end farm cruelty* campaign what are we really saying?

Let's think about this by asking what the answer would be in a human context.

We're feminists and we support the fundamental right of women to be equal to men. Would we congratulate someone for giving women equal pay, or suspending sexism, for only six months a year? We might accept those six months as being better than nothing, because it's a given that less suffering is better than more, but it wouldn't be our overall goal. The overall goal would be to continue pursuing equality and persuading people to recognise women have that right. The six-month win wouldn't warrant congratulating someone as having done something extraordinary because unequal pay and sexism remain very much a reality even if for half the year.

Similarly, when we support initiatives in favour of eating less meat or harming animals a bit less, despite our good intentions what we're really saying is eating just a little bit of meat, eggs, dairy or fish is okay and using animals is also okay as long as we do it gently. We compromise the fundamental rights of those animals who are outside of the immediate benefit of the campaign. We're lending our support to exploitative industries and we're rationalising animal use by others as long as it's carried out in some prescribed way.

You might be asking yourself, 'If we don't support these campaigns or initiatives how will we communicate to people we shouldn't be using animals?' That's a valid concern. To help us with this, we like to think about something Eleanor Roosevelt said: 'If you have to compromise, be sure to compromise up.'[16] That means if you have to compromise, make sure the compromise serves a larger purpose, not your own advancement, and doesn't sacrifice the beliefs you hold or the group you're concerned about.[17] When it comes to animals, we routinely compromise down.

We witnessed an example of what we mean by compromising down during an exchange between the owner of a vegan business and a customer. The vegan business is also involved in education and other charitable and community work. They do many good things. While talking about food, the owner said they were vegan and sometimes they ate animal products because they felt like it. The customer, an outspoken vegan involved in public activism, chose to reply it was fine for them to eat animal products now and again because of all the other good the owner was doing. Imagine an analogous scenario in a human context. Would we say, 'Oh, it's okay to be a misogynist when you fancy it because you're doing so much other good'? Probably not.

As vegans, we often accept these types of downward compromises. We lavish praise on people for giving up meat without a gentle reminder of the unfairness of dairy and eggs. We praise campaigns for larger cages for chickens because they mean some chickens get to live in less awful conditions, but these campaigns do nothing to stop demand for chicken and eggs in the first place. Perhaps we compromise down because we're ill prepared, unaccustomed to, or uncomfortable with, talking about our rejection of speciesism in terms of basic justice and fairness. We wouldn't talk about any other -ism in this way. Instead, when it comes to veganism, we hang on to any deceptively mild, benevolent-sounding words, without realising we're selling out the animals each time we do so; and, unconsciously, we're being speciesist when we accept poor substitutes for principles. Or perhaps we believe it's our only choice when it comes to talking about veganism or the fundamental rights of animals. Promoting campaigns and initiatives is relatively easy to achieve in relation to the overall goal of ending animal use and they're encouraging on a personal level because people feel they're doing something immediate and concrete. Ease of reaching a goal and those good feelings have everything to do with us and are only tangential to the animals who continue to suffer and die.

At an event where she was the guest, we heard Chimamanda Ngozi Adichie, renowned Nigerian writer and feminist, say, 'I know how quickly, in the face of sustained mediocrity, we collectively lower our standards, so that unacceptable things suddenly become not so bad.'[18] Adichie's words rang true in the context of why we often compromise down when it comes to animals. The sorts of campaigns and initiatives we've been considering seem to be mediocre attempts to avoid thinking about our actions or of their consequences. They use clever-sounding terms, like reducetarian or flexitarian, to praise us for continuing to kill and exploit animals for no good reason. Normalising these terms and ideas make them seem less harmful, but they're deadly. Our accepting these harmful notions will change very little for the animals. They'll continue to be the ones who pay the ultimate price with their lives. We must do better and compromise up because that's what we'd do in a human context.

We're not suggesting compromising up means scolding, verbally attacking, vilifying or being abusive towards anyone for their choices, even when they're unfair. Sometimes, discussing such matters is very difficult and can be impossible. Just as we wouldn't praise someone who says, 'I'm only a part-time sexist,' we can't praise reducetarians or flex... either. Perhaps silence is a better response if any meaningful exchange is impossible or too difficult. Silence can be powerful.

Simply, we believe veganism is something we owe animals because it's their right to be free from exploitation and owner-ship. Looking at things through that lens and the notion of compromising up makes us question a variety of approaches. For example, we suggest only protesting fur may make people comfortable wearing other animal products.[19] We also suggest that joining in calls for better treatment of animals raised for slaughter may continue to support consumer demand by making people feel less squeamish about the consequences of their food choices. By asking these tough questions and engaging in these conversations, we're merely examining and challenging practices and status quo so that we might effect the transformative change at the heart of veganism. We're all in this for the same reasons: it's always the animals.

Every fur coat, every cage, and every advertisement for the grass-fed, humanely raised animal product or the misinforma-tion about vegan diets stings the same way it stings all vegans. Every word we write, every conversation we have, it's with the animals in mind. We believe until veganism is on the lips and tongues of all those who want meaningful change for the for-gotten billions, *good enough* will continue to prevail with long enough lives, big enough cages, or kind enough killing.

A change in demand is key to begin edging towards fairness to animals. Take the success of faux leather leggings, for example. We see their success the same way we see the success of bacon. The popularity of each of these items – one vegan and the other not – is a result of people's demand for that item. Our product is all about. And what better way to a vegan world than through increasing vegans? This is compromising up! Being an vegan voice is useful in helping even one more use animal use. In turn, they may help another, con- ng to a virtuous circle. Surely this must have more far reaching and lasting consequences than the knowledge that all red carpets around the world will never again be graced with fur-wearing celebrities? Just one more vegan speaking up about the unspeakable actions against animals is *enough*, because it encompasses *everything*.

A NOTE ABOUT OUR HUMAN ANALOGIES

We're not equating human suffering and animal suffering. We're not minimising human suffering by drawing these parallels or making these analogies. We're also not replacing the human suffering and injustice we wilfully perpetrate on one another with the suffering and injustice we wilfully perpetrate on animals. They all exist simultaneously. We're using our understanding of human injustice and unfairness to expand our circle to include all sentient beings and help facilitate a deeper level of understanding regarding the impact and effects of our actions and our choices. We have no good reason not to include them.

Vegan or Plant-Based?

Being *plant-based* is a dietary trend emerging over the past few years. This buzzword is getting the kind of glib attention of any new fad diet, and is confusing just as many people. It's important to make the distinction between being vegan and plant-based.

What is a plant-based diet?

First and foremost, a plant-based diet is just that – *a diet*. It's grounded in good health, with adherents opting for high volumes of whole fruits and vegetables, as well as nuts, seeds and grains and low on so-called *processed* foods. It most commonly doesn't include meat, dairy or eggs. Often, it can be seen getting cosy with gluten free and organic labelled products.

People take up plant-based diets for several unique reasons, from illness prevention and weight loss, to saving money, oh! and having one more thing in common with one or other pop star.

You may be thinking, 'What's the problem here? No animals are harmed so there shouldn't be an issue with calling yourself plant-based, right?' While a plant-based meal might well be vegan, a person who *eats* a plant-based diet is often not. You may eat nothing but arugula for breakfast, lunch and dinner. If you then throw on a pair of leather shoes and head off to visit zoos and aquariums, you're not a vegan because you are still contributing to the objectification of animals. Many people who eat plant-based foods also won't necessarily eat exclusively vegan foods. You see, many vegan favourites aren't strictly plant-based at all. We're sure some vegans with a sweet tooth (*hi!*) will try to reassure you a second serving of Oreo crust chocolate tofu pie originates from plants after all, but there was a long time between the starting point and the delicious end product.

Plant-based is quite commonly mistaken for a *gentle* and

more marketable way of saying vegan. The similarities end at broccoli.

How does veganism differ?

For starters, veganism isn't a fad diet. Unlike *eating* plant-based, vegan is something you *become*. Being vegan entails a rejection of using animals, extending far past the plate or grocery store. Your clothing, cosmetics, cleaning products and other things we use daily are all also affected by a choice to follow veganism. And if sometimes being vegan means having to eat white bread because the only other buffet options have eggs in them, then so be it.

Vegans aren't *health nuts*. We don't avoid eating animal products because they're high in calories, just as we don't search for pleather pants because we heard leather ones are so last season. Of course, you'll find junk food eating plant-based people, and health-food eating vegans, but that's beyond the point.

Why do we care?

Remember that day when news broke of kale-T-shirt-wearing Beyoncé going vegan?[20] That day was simultaneously the best and worst for Queen B-appreciating vegans like us. No, Beyoncé didn't stop buying leather shoes, and she didn't write a song called 'Run the World (Vegans)'. She had simply switched to a plant-based diet for a while, and wanted the public to know how beneficial it was for her waistline. In advocating only for plant-based diets, we ignore the ethics underpinning veganism, which leads to missing the true point and purpose of veganism – to end injustice towards animals.

There's a clear distinction here: one is a diet and the other is an ethical choice centred on fairness. If you decided to try out a Jenny Craig plan, you'd never say, 'I'm a Jenny Craig.' You're not a gluten free or a paleo, you eat gluten free or are on a paleo diet. When people on a plant-based diet call themselves vegans while continuing to exploit animals, it makes it possible for people to assume all vegans are like that. We're not. And it masks some of the more horrific fundamental reasons why vegans are opposed to animal exploitation. Surely another jackfruit sandwich is easier to face than those horrors.

Can't we all just get along?

Sure, we can all rub elbows at a Whole Foods salad bar, admiring the selection of hummus and assorted veggies quite happily without scrapping. But truthfully, these individuals can be doing damage to animals, the planet and themselves on a plant-based diet as they would be on a non-vegan one. Rather than advocating people make small incremental changes, it's important vegans focus on the big, moral picture: *it's not fair to use animals.* When people are given information, they'll figure out how they can best apply it to their life. We won't applaud a celebrity for being against hunting while they simultaneously continue to eat animal products, and we won't pat the backs of people who think refraining from eating animal products makes it somehow okay that we don't question if they continue in any other way to use animals.

Don't get too upset. We're aware of the potential here. I mean, if people are comfortable with trading steaks for green smoothies, they must have the capacity to care and possess a ton of patience. All we ask the plant-based individuals is to consider the underlying moral issues surrounding all forms of animal exploitation other than food. We ask the non-vegans in our life to stop assuming we're vegan for the v-shaped cuts in our abdominals or well-defined bodies. We go boxing for those bad boys.

Eating a plant-based diet has many benefits. Choosing veganism can make a difference in more than just your own life.

A Framework for Analysing Animal Issues

When faced with answering any question about animal issues or veganism, we generally follow this framework:

- **Identify what the issues or problems are, remembering there may be more than one.**
  When thinking about any issue relating to justice or fairness, the following mental picture may be helpful: imagine a wheel, where the group who is at the heart of the fairness or justice issue forms the hub and all the other issues are the spokes. The spokes emanate from the hub. The spokes and the hub are simultaneously individual and interconnected. Start thinking about the problem from the hub and then proceed to each issue, or spoke, in relation to how it affects the hub.

- **Ask yourself, 'What's at stake?'**

  And think about if there's any morally relevant reason to treat this situation differently than if it were in a human context. For example, think back to the two analogies we made earlier about wool and human hair and eat less meat and be less sexist. Would we use the hair or the slogan in a human context? No, because lives and fairness are at stake. And the same applies in the animal context. Alternatively, we're not going to give animals the right to vote no matter how old they are because they can't engage with politics like adult people can. In this case, the difference between us and them is morally relevant. Sure, it sounds absurd, perfectly illustrating our point.

- **Apply the principle(s) to the situation and try to figure out how they would work.**

  It's critical to keep the animals as the focus of any discussion about animal use and veganism. Veganism isn't about us. *We* aren't the focus of our veganism. Of course, some aspects of veganism are about people. It's just never *all* about humans. We're not the ones being used as objects or losing our lives for the benefit of another animal species.

When we discuss issues we fully understand, our voices become a very powerful tool because we deliver our message in our own simple and authentic manner, which may give us a good chance to connect with others around us. We may not convince people all the time. At the very least, we'll plant the best and strongest seeds possible from which fruitful future conversations or actions may arise.

Throughout this book, and particularly in the final chapter, you'll find thought experiments and situations challenging you to consider a different viewpoint related to veganism. Many of them can be answered by asking, 'What would be the answer in a human context?' Sometimes, there won't be a satisfactory answer. Other times, the answer will highlight or bring up other injustices and unfairness in our world. This is okay, and we encourage you to explore the issues in deeper contemplation. Thinking through the hard questions that may be difficult to resolve is part of evolving and striving for justice and fairness for all. There's no place for complacency when it comes to bringing about social and moral change. And remember, if the answer is to *compromise up* when it comes to the fundamental rights of humans, then it also has to be to *compromise up* when it comes to the fundamental rights of animals.

Chapter 1 Takeaways

- Vegans reject speciesism and must by logical extension also reject and oppose all other forms of bigotry.
- To the extent possible and practicable, vegans avoid using animals for food, clothing, entertainment or any other purpose.
- We have no morally relevant reason for treating animals differently when it comes to the essential right to be free from exploitation. Using animals is the root of the problem: animals are considered property under laws the world over, whether they're wild, on a farm or in your home. The goal of abolishing the legal notion of animals as property is fundamental.
- Are you faced with an animal-ethics-related problem or question? If so, find the analogy in a human context, see if it works or why it doesn't, and you'll find a solution.

CHAPTER 2

Live and Love Vegan

How does veganism affect our daily, work, love, social or family life, or our relationship to animals in the home, and is there room for us to speak clearly about veganism?

Unlike elsewhere in this work, some of these very personal essays speak only from the viewpoint of the authors as individuals.

Vegans Don't Need Capes

The heroism of veganism is overstated.

We get asked if it's true if you'll lose weight, or live longer, and if 100 animals will be spared because of you. People inquire as to whether we've always had clear skin, the endurance to run, or the ability to craft social-media-worthy meals. 'Oh,' people exclaim upon the news of how we live, 'that's really amazing. I wish I could do that.'

We're not sure how, but veganism has been inappropriately characterised as a spandex-wearing vigilante who isn't only saving animals, water and land, but ourselves. Veganism has been made out to be the near impossible answer to all of life's most fearsome villains, and the sometimes-insurmountable barriers to the freedom, body size, or comfort we expect from it. *You've done your part; you had a vegan chocolate-chip cookie today.*

Veganism isn't the light at the end of the tunnel, or the rope that's going to get you out of your hole. It won't illuminate darkness with hints of glitter, or give you the energy to pretend you're now the indestructible force, gleaming poster child or leading example this world needs.

Despite what social media tells us, veganism won't make you perfect, encased in a bubble of kale and green smoothies. You'll still choke on water. Pain and sadness will still find a way into your depths. You aren't suddenly able to magically overcome what can harm you.

At times, it won't just be the menu stacked against you. Being unable to find a wool-free formal suit might stir up something in you. The way they always forget to include you in the office treat day will sting more than the stuck tongue at the end of a carmine-coloured popsicle. You'll feel the weight of every single person who decides veganism is too hard, and wonder for yourself if it truly is.

You'll think of every docked tail, every clipped beak; the farm and domestic animals without plush beds to dream on, and those who have whips and hot stage lights for homes. You'll imagine the eyes and cries of small faces who, despite never asking to be born, have found themselves to be a pawn in this unfair game, where a biased few decide the fate of the many innocents.

You might even wonder how they see *you* as a pawn. How they managed to first make you believe what we all do is right, and then how they work to make us believe we don't belong when we don't take part. It won't be as straightforward as a bumper sticker slogan or a catchphrase. It will be something constantly begging you to pay attention, be present, make good choices and stand up, go again, and improve.

It's not about how you'll feel, or how you'll do. It's never been about whether your body will respond or how your mind will fare. You aren't on a 21-day challenge to perfection, to being able to slide into that cape with the effort and grace that shows everyone you're infallible. Being vegan isn't about *you*.

Being vegan won't get you the girl, the boy, the job or the celebrity status. It doesn't exist for your posts, scrapbooks or holidays. It's not the unbelievable feat of the hero who bounds from rooftop to rooftop, sending shockwaves down into the homes of everyone around you.

Then again, the heroism of veganism is understated.

Veganism makes you feel a bit less small, like maybe you have the strength and speed to tackle some of the horror in the dark alleys of the world. It's a very small piece of your puzzle, helping you to complete the full picture of your own personhood. You might not get to feel the joy of an embrace from a rescued animal, but you'll also not have to suffer knowing you're wearing what's been taken from them. Seeing the windows of a butcher shop may remain a thorn in your side, but it's a powerful sword tucked neatly against your other hip. Your ability to fight against what's expected will need to be understood, questioned, shared. And you'll get to choose exactly how you explain veganism to others.

You're not the misery of animal exploitation and its death, fear, hate, pain, separation, loneliness, greed, mistrust, illusions, deceptions, horror, entrapment and shackling. You're not burdened to trudge on a path forged for you by someone else, bought and sold and bought again in a vicious cycle that once forced you to be a part of the process.

You may look the same, feel the same and act the same, but you're not the same.

You're already everything that veganism promises: its goodness, love, caring, understanding, patience and perseverance. You know it's not about you but about the animals, and you do it because it's the right thing to do. And without fanfare, you're a hero. Heroes aren't their outfits, their habits or their longevity. Heroes aren't revered for never being hurt or frightened. Heroes are heroes because they choose to recognise the needs of another, and then they act upon them accordingly.

You are veganism. You choose to take that first step in a lifetime of movement towards good.

Serves Them Right!

When there's an animal involved in a conflict with humans, we sometimes hear people, vegan or not, rejoice in human suffering or withhold sympathy for the people involved in the situation.

It's the *serves them right!* mentality and response. Think of the toreador getting gored by a bull or the hunter getting shot, or the non-vegan contracting a diet-related disease.

We read an article about most chicken products in the UK containing the E.coli bacterium and heard someone say they would withhold sympathy from the unfortunate infected humans, siding with the chickens. They would choose to celebrate the human suffering because they believe the person brought that suffering upon themselves by consuming chicken. While we understand the reaction, we ask this: why rejoice in human suffering at all? The attitude doesn't advance any cause. Bacterial justice serves no purpose other than self-indulgent *Schadenfreude*. And what if bacterial justice felled someone we loved? Or even one of us before we went vegan?

There's no need to rejoice in others' suffering. We're advocating for the end of suffering in the first place and everyone deserves that. Our hearts and minds are big enough to have room for all. We can at least try to be approachable, taking the opportunity to talk with people about the sorrow or discomfort they feel. We can point out those feelings for the animals mean they already understand the basics of veganism. We might also help to connect the dots to the origins of the disease, showing how a vegan diet might avoid such diseases and more. There's an opportunity to showcase how veganism is a way to deal with injustice and we can start demonstrating that by being the best spokesperson for veganism we can.

Vegansexualism

Is anyone else uncomfortable with the idea of non-vegans discussing who vegans should and shouldn't sleep with?

Vice shared a piece called 'Inside the World of "Vegansexualism" – the Vegans Who Only Date Other Vegans', making us want to cross our legs a little tighter.[1] The exploration of how vegans express their sexuality isn't new.[2] What's new and newsworthy, as the number of vegans increases, is looking into how this sexual preference is evolving. Whether they're discussing bodily fluids or sharing an entree at a blind date, there's really no mystery to uncover in the preferences of vegans to flock together. And there's *nothing* wrong with that.

The discussion began back in 2007, when a curious New Zealand doctor surveyed 157 vegans and vegetarians on cruelty-free living and didn't sugar coat the sex questions. Reasonably, dead-animal breath ranked high as a reason a vegan would avoid dating a non-vegan. With the vegan population rising, *Vice* proposed that the world must be crawling with vegansexuals by now. Because the term hasn't yet climbed to the ranks of metrosexual or even tacosexual, berating vegans for ranking their morality above their sexual escapades seems trivial.

The author interviewed a handful of vegans, pulling responses fitting the *easy-going* or *militant* vegan stereotypes to a tee. A participant named Kirilee made it simple and said, 'An environmentalist wouldn't be involved with a coal miner.' Another participant named Ben quickly contradicted her by claiming, 'I could be in a relationship with any non-vegan. My belief is it's best to lead by example rather than preaching my personal views.' Save for compromising and being stuck with salad, he didn't see the problem. These two camps very accurately represent the group, like Ben, who believes veganism is about themselves (a diet for health, the earth, etc.) and their contrasting comrades like Kirilee, who consider veganism a moral imperative (*yo!*). One highlights veganism as something *they're* doing, thus making it unnecessary for their partner to partake. The other believes veganism is about the victim, and couldn't comfortably bed anyone who currently takes part in the exploitation. Again, it's not new material. No matter the popularity of veganism, vegans are going to be grilled for making choices other than normative ones, simply because veganism is still new to much of the public and observers heavily scrutinise it with a biased lens.

Some commenters upped the ante by calling non-vegan bodies *cemeteries*. They described the natural bodily scent of carnivores as unpleasant for vegans. We believe this is an emotional response. After all, most people have an ordinary sense of smell and we can't detect a scent of dead animals mingling with a floral perfume. Nevertheless, it's understandable we might think of not being vegan as a turnoff.

This type of thinking only leads us back to a carousel of physical traits and habits as our driving factors for partner selection, instead of the driver being our potential partner's ethics. We believe such superficial drivers make it all too easy for someone to misjudge a potential vegan partner if they're basing the judgment on preconceived ideas of what a vegan might be like – in this case, great-smelling.

When *Vice* said, 'Just because you don't want to eat meat, doesn't mean you have to shut out anyone who does', they diminish the significance of veganism, and categorise it as being as frivolous as having a preference in a partner's hair colour or physique. They negate whether we're comfortable getting into someone's leather-seated car, their silk sheets, and if we'd be happy to meet up with them at the zoo for a date, not to mention their food choices day in and day out. Dating a non-vegan is more than what they bring to your family potluck, just as dating a vegan is more than how they should look, act or – *ick* – taste. Exploration of sexuality doesn't need to be conflated with veganism in mainstream conversation, and vegansexuals need not be villainized or fetishized.

Still, we'll never understand vegans who *actively* seek out non-vegan partnerships.[3] While the premise of converting those close to us is often unjustly recommended as the only way, partnerships are best formed when people are themselves, and when ethical identity is tied to issues and not individuals. We don't think the conversation should swirl around what non-vegans think vegans should do. Instead, we should discuss the resources available to vegans who wish to date other vegans, and the materials to help illustrate why we need veganism. Although we know sex sells, there's absolutely nothing sexy about compromising our own integrity and mental health in the pursuit of acceptance, physical gratification or a partner. While many readers may have had the experience of helping guide a non-vegan to a full transition, it should still be the overwhelming majority (not the originally represented 60%) who put veganism at the top of their list of partner-wants. And we shouldn't feel shamed or singled out for doing so.

Our Journey and Advocacy

Each of us came to veganism as a result of some experience. We might have watched a film, read a book, had a conversation, participated in a vegan challenge, or been influenced by an advertising campaign. We might have gone through a prolonged thought process or had concerns about our health or the environment. Perhaps we had a sudden revelation, a moment of clarity, or made a connection between our food, clothing or other choices and their devastating repercussions. It may have taken us years to go vegan or we might have made that choice early on in our lives. We might have observed Meatless Mondays for a time. We might even have been vegetarian before realising dairy and eggs were the results of just as much exploitation and death as any meat. These experiences are valid and important because they make up our individual and collective histories. They're part of our life's story, making it easier for us to relate to others and how they may be thinking about or approaching veganism. The journey per se has no impact on the ethical message underpinning veganism.

Whether directly or by implication, all vegans acknowledge we were misguided prior to going vegan. Every vegan we've ever met has said something like, 'It's the best thing I ever did' or 'I wish I'd done it sooner', usually both. But when it comes to advocating for veganism, often we rely on a subjective journey to limit our discussions. Our personal experiences are valuable because we understand where non-vegans are coming from. They're useful tools for us to thoughtfully and kindly communicate shared experiences, enabling us to educate, banish misconceptions, answer questions and demystify veganism. However, there is no reason these should be the baseline from which we determine whether we discuss veganism in the first place. We've witnessed vegans shy away from having discussions about veganism with non-vegans only because they too were non-vegan at some point.

We can use our experiences to create connections with others. For example, when someone learns we're vegan, they often nod approvingly and proceed to tell us they no longer eat a particular animal, usually cows, or they've cut down consuming animal products. These acknowledgments may signal a certain level of receptivity and understanding. Depending on the rest of the interaction, we take the opportunity to be supportive of their behaviour and to gently nudge their thought process. We might ask why they're making distinctions between animals or why they're cutting back instead of going vegan. We might also just simply say what they're doing is good and we hope they'll one day go vegan. If the conversation continues, we always make clear that although doing less harm is better than doing more, the goal is veganism. Some will be receptive to this and some won't. Like with any moral choice, it's up to each of us to decide what to do with the information once it's been presented to us. Nevertheless, these conversations often lead to further discussions, which is never a bad thing. Many people would've gone vegan sooner if they had understood the ethical implications of veganism, instead of the frequent calls to only reduce consumption or to choose animal products with higher standards of welfare. We know we would have.

How Being Straight Edge Prepared Me for Veganism

I went straight edge early into my adulthood.[4] Straight edge is a philosophy promoting self-respect, which emerged as a counterpoint to the excesses of punk culture. Being straight edge demands we cast off a variety of social norms, including the consumption of drugs and alcohol. While some choose to exclude promiscuity and include animal rights in their straight-edge practices, I originally saw the latter as a very personal choice. It would be many years before I once again made myself a black sheep of my family and an outsider in my social circles by choosing to go vegan. Later, I discovered other straight-edge people consider veganism as fundamental to the concept as abstinence from intoxicants.

Reflecting on both choices, I can see now how being straight edge prepared me for going vegan. The aggression, curiosity, solidarity and conflicts I was met with in both transitions were practically the same. So was the desire to live without violence.

In my family, like in so many others, alcohol was used in celebration, religious ritual, or simply at the end of a long day. It seemed one was expected to consume alcohol as a release, and a big part of my unease was rooted in the way people around me used it as a crutch. When I would say 'no thanks' as a bottle of wine was passed around, I was met with a confused audience. Many times, people would bargain for me to try it, or do their best to convince me they deserved it as a reward for something they did or dealt with during the day. Despite the puzzled looks or the aggressive responses from some, others were equally curious or praised me for my choice. Some argued they could never eschew alcohol, while simultaneously acknowledging I was doing the right thing. I got a lot of *good-for-you*s.

Sound familiar?

When I gave up meat, the same things happened. I would pass on whatever meat was placed in front of me and people would either argue or praise. All the years I had spent saying no to drinks were a foreshadowing of what would happen when I said no to meat. Later, I would discover the strong connection between choosing to be straight edge and choosing veganism.

Socially, it wasn't always easy feeling like an outsider. As my friends and I grew up, the presence of drugs, and experimentation with a variety of substances, only heightened. I made it through university, the dorm rooms, the parties, the relationships, and was still sure of who I wanted to be, and even more clearly what I didn't want to be a part of. That's when it became easier to stop participating in events where I knew drugs and alcohol would be heavily present, admittedly at the sacrifice of some people who didn't see things like I did.

I struggled with the same obstacles when I went vegan. Initially, I was happy to share a table with someone dining on animal products. Then slowly, I found myself avoiding it as much as possible. Consequently, I gradually lost some of the people in my life who weren't heading in the same direction.

Those who care about me respect my choices, and I theirs. Not sharing some experiences, especially the most common ones around dining tables, removes a commonality people rely upon, consciously or unconsciously, to facilitate feelings of closeness and companionship. I've noticed being the person who doesn't want to party falls in line with the same responses as being the person who doesn't want to join in on bacon fandom. It's never been about my not liking people who drink or smoke, but an aversion to the act. It's the same with non-vegans. I don't dislike them, but I do dislike the continued choice to consume animals. As a straight-edge person, I avoid living in a way destructive to myself and those around me. This also defines veganism for me. I want to be free from the destructive forces of substances, and I want that same freedom from destructive forces for the animals.

Because veganism and straight edge are so similar, people often ask if my straight edge stems from ethics. With my veganism being first and foremost for the animals, and not for reasons of health or the environment, I'm not put off by this assumption. Truthfully, my discomfort with drugs and alcohol doesn't come close to my strong feelings about animal use. In that respect, experiencing life through the lens of being straight edge was a softer step than going vegan. The difference is: one affects me on a small scale, and the other goes well beyond my own needs. On the one hand, while some-one's choice to drink or do drugs can affect those closest around them, the choice primarily and directly affects them-selves (we're leaving aside the very real and potentially devas-tating consequences of the drug trade on a variety of people who are involved in it). On the other hand, choosing to use animal products always goes beyond oneself because it's unavoidably connected to the death of an animal too. Thus, in the case of animal-based foods, the consequences of one person's actions aren't purely individual.

Do I think vegans need to be straight edge? Not necessarily. Can people in the straight-edge community stand to include veganism? Oh, hell yes.

While it's not uncommon to see both co-existing, I think people who already understand the obstacles presented by abstaining from drugs and alcohol will have an easier time transitioning to veganism. Eating, dressing and basing your consumerism on veganism is never as difficult as the interac-tions it asks us to have with people on the other side. And if someone cares deeply for themselves and the people around them, it's not peculiar to think they should add animals into this consideration too.

Being both straight edge and vegan, I have learned to align myself with the things I believe in. The similarities are clear, and the choice not to follow conventions is always going to be met with suspicion. When it comes to living my best life for myself and for others, I see being vegan or straight edge as interchangeable. Living a life of non-violence starts with me, and extends out to all sentient beings.

Why Did I Go Vegan in My Forties?

About thirty years ago I had become vegetarian. I subsequently transitioned to being vegan. At that point, I didn't understand the ethics underpinning veganism. So, I ruefully admit, I didn't stick to it.

My family would make everything from scratch. From a very young age, my father, a philosopher and despite being non-vegan, taught me there's no difference between our non-human animal companions and those we kill for food. During my vegetarian and vegan phase all those years ago, I learned to cook for myself.

As I matured, I couldn't bear to see injustices or anyone being mistreated. I cared about the environment too. I keenly felt the wonder and fleeting nature of life, especially after experiencing the untimely death of two young friends.[5] And I wanted love to win the day for everyone no matter their sexual orientation. Despite all this, I didn't fully understand how all injustice is connected, including what I chose to eat. At that point in my life, I knew no vegans and I believed veganism was only a diet. As a diet, I made it very restrictive. I only focused on its impact on myself and I held squishy New Age-y notions about consuming animals.

Eventually, I got bored with myself and my muddy thinking about my food choices. I saw no point in continuing being vegan. So, I lapsed. I changed my diet and went on to consume organic and humane animal products, thinking those labels made a marked difference (they don't).

Then, something happened several years ago.

My husband and I decided to try in vitro fertilisation (IVF).

We knew it was a long shot (a 75% chance of failure). We thought we'd give it one go. The process was brutal and unforgiving, both physically and mentally. You're constantly going to see a doctor, having blood work daily, arriving at the lab super early in the morning to minimise disruption to your day, and you get to inject yourself in the abdomen with all sorts of drugs, which I did in the most unlikely places, including the toilets in various offices, cafés, restaurants, theatres and museums in London. Good times. Despite knowing the odds are never in your favour, there's a point when you start believing it will work.

What really struck me during the process was being in the doctor's office with all those women who were there for the sole reason of becoming mothers. We all had a shared purpose. Despite this hope, I felt unease because I had a recurring mental image of a butcher shop. There was a kind of objectification of our bodies as machines, with a relentless queuing, waiting, prodding and testing and, through it all, a palpable unease; also fear and sorrow. Of course, it wasn't a butcher shop, and the doctors and nurses I met were kind and caring. Despite there being no death or cruelty in what I was experiencing, I couldn't help how I perceived it. That mental image resonated once more, when I later read Carol J. Adams' *The Sexual Politics of Meat*.[6] Broadly, the work focuses on the objectification of women and food animals.

Despite this unease, I kept at the process. Throughout, I maintained my almost daily running routine, which gave me time to think. I thought a lot about IVF, my feelings about it, whether it would work, why we were there, and whether procreating was even the right thing to do. In the end, IVF didn't work for us and we were okay with that. We were disappointed, of course, but weren't going to let it dictate our life.

IVF did have one significant and unintended consequence that changed everything.

During one morning's routine, a question occurred to me: how is it possible for cows to express milk on demand when humans only do that after we've given birth? The answer is now as obvious as can be: they can't! That answer had never occurred to me before.

Then my thoughts turned to all those women, myself included, sat waiting for IVF treatment, hoping to one day be able to give birth. There we all were, in all our human privilege of making reproductive choices, while we were taking babies away from other females with impunity.

I couldn't imagine anyone wanting to do that to a mother. The horror was unfathomable. But that's what we do on a mass scale every day. We use cows as reproductive machines for our benefit, whilst simultaneously taking away their babies. At that moment, the mental image I had had at the clinic of being in a butcher shop came flooding back to me. This time, I felt as if I were the butcher. How could we be so heartless, I thought? How could we be so selfish in doing whatever we could to give birth to children of our own and then perpetrating such horrors on a new mother? How could I, as a feminist, do this to another female? It went against everything I believed was important.

These realisations hit me like a baseball bat slugged across my stomach. They stopped me in my tracks and at that very moment I became vegan. I knew I had to. Overnight, I got rid of all the non-vegan food in the house and, over time, I replaced non-vegan clothes, shoes and household items.

From that moment, I educated myself. I researched and learned about the heart-rending practices of all dairy farms and about egg-laying hens in hatcheries. I became increasingly interested in the effect of these industries upon the environment, about the unimaginable hell for the animals, and the vast scale of it all, which was simultaneously mind-bending and deeply distressing. No matter how switched on or culturally and politically aware I felt I was at the time, I had never thought about any of these issues. I realised we're conditioned to never stop and think about any of this because it's all around us and it's the norm; it's systemic.

The easiest part was the food. I saw how many websites, blogs and recipe books existed already. I spent a bit of time reading them and trying a variety of recipes and cooking techniques. I got used to reading labels. I was surprised to see how many items contained a needless animal product (why do we need milk powder in some brands of crisps?!). I never doubted it was a healthy choice because I knew most of our chronic diseases come from our consumption of animal products. The tough part was dealing with others who were sometimes hostile to my shift. This time was different than when I had gone vegan in my twenties. This time, I had read and understood the reasons for going vegan and the ethics, so I wasn't going to be put off.

People still ask me whether I miss animal products, particularly cheese or bacon. The answer is always no. I feel like I've switched off a lamp in a well-lit room. I don't miss that light; I didn't need it to begin with. There are plenty of other sources of light to illuminate my way, and by that, I mean there are loads of yummy things to eat which don't involve another's suffering and death. I feel liberated. I have chosen to let love and fairness win the day, every day. There's nothing to be missed, except not doing it sooner.

The Rocky Road to My Partner Going Vegan

When I went vegan, my first real challenge was telling my partner. He had been vegetarian for most of his life, but he ate fish, which annoyed me no end. During one of our early dates, I couldn't help reminding him that fish aren't vegetables. Yep, I said that! I suppose this alone should've been enough notice for him as to what kind of character I was going to be. He stuck around anyway. But Roger loved dairy cheese.

Our first discussion about going vegan resulted in a heated argument one evening at our dining table. His position was dairy cheese was one of the few pleasures of life. I agreed with him it tasted good. I countered that liking how something tastes isn't a good reason to exploit and kill cows, reminding him they're slaughtered in the same slaughterhouses used to produce meat. We went on from there; a back and forth of all the possible arguments for and against. What Roger said to me at the end was one of the most significant things he had, or has ever, said to me: 'We cannot diverge on a moral issue. That's too big.'

Although he disagreed with me, and I had no idea if he was ever going to change his mind, I appreciated he understood immediately the magnitude of what we were discussing. Despite the storminess between us, I loved him much more for having the heart to understand the fundamental nature of the issue and having the courage to say it. I was worried about where this would lead; I also knew I could no longer buy, handle or cook any non-vegan food. I resolved to do my best to discuss the issue and the reasons with him whenever it felt right.

At home, we always ate vegan food. When we went out together, he always ordered the vegan option. I didn't know what he ate when we weren't together and I didn't ask. It wasn't my place to do so, even though I so wanted to understand his thinking. I let it be. I just kept on keeping on. I prepared good vegan food, found vegan restaurants or vegan options at non-vegan restaurants for us to try, and lived my vegan life by example. We discussed veganism now and again and, often, the conversation got heated or contentious. I realised it wasn't going to be an easy road to vegan harmony.

Several months after the first conversation, I hosted a milestone birthday party for him, complete with vegan Italian food, cheeses, cake and drinks. On the e-invites I even asked if guests were bringing gifts to please ensure they were vegan-friendly. Many of his friends and colleagues attended from various parts of the UK and it was the first time many of them had been exposed to either vegans or vegan food, or both! I was anxious, but secure in my decision, and I knew the food was going to be delicious. At some point while I was refilling someone's glass and checking on a guest, I overheard Roger reply to a friend who had asked him if he'd gone vegan too. I'm pretty sure I turned to stone that instant! Roger's reply was yes, he had, because there was no reason not to.

I pretended I hadn't heard his reply and kept making the rounds among the guests. All I wanted to do was weep with joy and relief. I know I'm very fortunate he also chose veganism, and I don't take his companionship for granted.

I don't know what would've happened had he never gone vegan. I know my initial struggles aren't unique; many people struggle with non-vegan partners. As with any other non-vegan, living by example and talking about veganism are the only things we can do. Whether others choose veganism is up to them. My hope in sharing this about my life is to inspire others to embrace their veganism and to never stop discussing it whenever possible because we just don't know when someone will be ready to listen and make the change.

Veganism and Yoga

Yoga means a lot of things to a lot of different people. From exercise to therapy, the practice of unfurling one's mat has the potential to shape the way a person feels not just throughout their practice or their day, but throughout their life. As the average North American studio model for teaching yoga has shifted from just exercise to include education (as a yoga instructor, I say, '*yay!*'), non-vegan yoga educators ignore the practice of non-violence, a concept that's inherent in yoga philosophy.

Many yoga studios emphasise how good you can feel and look from adopting a regular yoga practice, and that couldn't be truer. Others invite students to sit with stillness and cultivate a healthier relationship with their thoughts, which is also amazing. However, there often isn't time to get into the philosophical or cultural roots of yoga. Most of us won't be exposed to these at all unless we take a teacher training course. So why is it we, as yoga educators, finally get to learn the philosophy behind yoga and then we ignore one of its critical components in our daily life?

One of the most commonly followed ancient texts, the *Yoga Sutras of Patanjali*,[7] and its outline of the eight limbs of yoga, breaks down what we aim to do in yoga and what will happen as a result. Of these eight limbs, the very first is yamas, understood to be our social contract or universal moralities. And the core principle of yamas, which we learn before ever even holding a downward dog pose, is ahimsa, or universal non-violence.

Although ahimsa is often interpreted in many ways, it's understood to mean *refraining from violent words, actions, and even abstaining from violent thoughts*. Imagine my excitement, naively thinking everyone in our forty-plus class of yoga teachers in training were going to go vegan. Now, we wouldn't need a celebrity vegan; we would have ancient teachings to support us!

Unfortunately, as with all seemingly difficult things, people decide to only take what they like and want from yoga, and leave the rest behind. In this case, instructors often urge not surrendering to road rage or not pushing yourself too far to land a headstand, but they leave out the billions of farm and trillion aquatic animals we needlessly kill each year for human use. Is it fair to take on the insurmountable task of facilitating a spiritual connection while breaking between classes for a lunch comprised of, well, edible forms of violence? Do we contradict our own hard work by striving for a more yogic society, while giving permission to participate in perhaps the least yoga thing people regularly do – support causing violence and death to a mind-numbing number of animals every single minute of every day?

With 500 hours of yoga education under my belt, I often feel the tension between sharing the *whole* practice including ahimsa, and the reality of only being able to share the *marketable* parts. Admittedly, when I'm in the studio leading a class full of yogis, I fear overstepping the line between encouraging veganism and potentially making non-vegans feel unwelcome. I want to do the former while avoiding the latter, of course, and I continually seek the inspiration and compassion to be as inclusive as possible.

I often think about a mantra I was taught by one of the wisest teachers I ever had:

lokah samastah sukhino bhavantu – May all beings everywhere be happy and free, and may my thoughts and my actions somehow contribute to that freedom for all.[8]

It's impossible to devote ourselves to this intention for universal good if we continue to participate in animal cruelty, denying so many beings a basic happiness and freedom. I believe all people have goodness in them and the desire to love. Sharing the compassion inherent in veganism, while practising yoga in a studio full of other open-minded, peace-promoting and loving individuals, is an extraordinary prospect. As eternal students, I hope yoga educators who aren't vegan might reconsider what it means to practise ahimsa both on and off the mat.

Libby: An Argument for Rescuing Animals

In September 2015, we were united with Libby, a 10 lb rabbit with a love for lounging on the couch. She was in desperate need of a new home after having escaped from a rabbit meat farm. Upon reading a call to action, it didn't take long for us to fill out the application, clear our spare bedroom, and get ourselves ready for our new roommate. Since then, we've grown inseparable from our girl, as most people do with their pets. As our friends and family came to meet her, one by one, they asked why we didn't get a smaller rabbit, a white rabbit, or a floppy-eared rabbit. They wanted to know why her, and our answer was always clear and simple: because she needed a good home and we had one to offer. We truly believe in the value of rescuing animals, something that is a hot button topic for many vegans and non-vegans alike. When we consider the lives of our pets as companionship and not as ownership, it's easy to move away from the pet store and breeding models, and towards adoption, which is a more ethical approach to finding companion animals.

In North America, there's a serious overpopulation of animals in shelters. With breeders, puppy mills and pet stores profiting from the popularity of trendy pets, there are a staggering number of animals sent to kennels, shelters and to their deaths. If we look just at dogs, 5,500 are killed in shelters across the USA each day. Five and a half thousand dogs per day! That number is overwhelming, to say the least. Just imagine all dogs, cats and small domestic animals combined. Suddenly, all the sentimental and heart-wrenching Sarah McLachlan advertisements in the world don't begin to scratch the surface.[9] In breaking down myths involving breeds, pet stores and animal emotional stability, we hope to inspire you to make the difference in the life of an animal in need instead of contributing to the production of new ones.

Animals are bred in different ways to suit different purposes. In Libby's case, she is half Flemish giant – the largest breed of rabbit. They're an obvious choice in the meat and fur industries. They don't typically make first-choice pets. It's usually around Easter when the small, dainty and docile rabbits are bred to be marketed to children.

In the case of dogs, you don't have to walk far before encountering a French bulldog, arguably one of the most designer dog breeds currently in existence. Or take pugs, for example. They're prone to a slew of problems as a result of selective breeding and have developed health issues related to progressively flatter faces. This trait doesn't serve the animal. It only appeals to humans. The trendiness of an animal means many dogs not fitting the mould are going to lose by comparison. Imagine if we all applied that same mentality to children and would only keep those who turned out looking a desired way. Or worse, if we somehow genetically engineered ways to alter our children's appearances, no matter the cost to their health. Shortening the lifespan or complicating the functions of an animal's life to suit our aesthetics is an often-unseen flip side to our breed and species obsessions when it comes to pets and companion animals.

Another common deception is the pet store. As we pass by store windows, we can get that feeling of needing to rescue the creature behind the glass. The thing is, for each animal *rescued* from a pet store, another will fill their place. When breeders and mills have a market for their animals, they continue to fill the demand. So how do pet stores help drive demand? By perpetuating the myths of pure-bred animals being the best or only puppies being the cutest dogs in the world.

These myths cast another long shadow on shelters, which are portrayed as dark and dingy homes full of middle-aged and elderly animals, too sick for people to afford to adopt or care for them. By comparison, breeders show happy animals all over their shiny websites. If we can see past the marketing breeders do to keep their businesses afloat, we'll be able to recognise that it's the animals up for adoption who should be *most* sought after.

Often, people rule out rescuing altogether in favour of having more information about an animal's upbringing. Libby showed some signs of aggression, fearing people when she was backed into corners. Much like with a frightened person, patience and love are the recipe for animals who have had a rough start. What if we cast people out for having had an emotional breakdown? For not listening to us? For making mistakes? Instead of just focusing on the traits or habits need-ing extra attention, rescues should be celebrated for having established personalities, quirks, and for commonly being already spayed or neutered and waste trained. When people look at animals as companions, and not as property, they can learn to accept and work with who they are.

Some days, we watch Libby as she energetically bounds from one corner of the room to the other, and we find it impossible to imagine her in the back of a small cage. Amaz-ingly, her spirit has already helped many people in our life make the connection between their dinner and the incredible animal they could have been (she's a vegan advocate, obviously). When we focus on picking and choosing our animals from people who design and sell them to us, we can lose sight of what sharing our homes with animals really offers. If we open ourselves to caring about the mass number of animals already existing, we end up finding the love, companionship and mutual growth we desire from the relationship in the first place. If you're ready to bring a pet into your home, consider Libby, and find a sanctuary, shelter or rescue in your area.

Honey Isn't Ours

Honey is sometimes at the heart of needlessly heated and prolonged debates. This seems odd because it's obviously a product made by bees for their own use, not ours. We have no need for it, and there are many substitutes. Whether honey consumption is ethical takes us back to basics and requires we consider *what would be the answer in a human context.*

Imagine you live in a small village in the mountains far from all food shops. Your village gets snowed in during winter, without a possibility of you leaving the house. During summer, you work your tail off to prepare all types of canned, pickled and smoked foods, you buy provisions and freeze them, and you stash it all away so you can eat during winter. Suddenly, your neighbour, who has plenty of their own food, believes yours is somehow magical and health-enhancing. They come along, throw a smoke bomb in your house, take most of your food away and replace it with sugared water. You may or may not survive winter on sugared water and whatever stores of your own food they have left you with. Then while stealing your food, your neighbour accidentally kills one or more members of your family and there's nothing you can do about it because your neighbour is much stronger than you in every way.

This is the reality of honey. Whether individually or commercially produced, honey isn't a harmless product. In commercial production, bees are specifically bred to increase honey yields, which narrows the genetic pool of all bee species, leaving them susceptible to disease and colony death. In addition, during maintenance of the hives, it's possible to accidentally kill bees, no matter how carefully a keeper handles the box or frames.[10] After the honey harvest, many commercial keepers kill a portion of their bees to keep their costs low.[11]

Honey is the food bees produce to feed themselves during the winter months. People have plenty of other sweeteners from which to choose, and all come from plants, including syrups made from apples, maple, sorghum, barley malt, brown rice, agave, coconut and dandelion, as well as molasses and even commercial vegan honeys.[12] We have no additional health or beauty-related need for honey, and all its purported beneficial attributes are plentiful in plant sources.[13] It's not a magic potion curing disease any more than any other thick, sugary syrup mixed into a hot liquid. It's neither our food nor our medicine.[14] Our only reasons for using honey are arbitrary and self-serving, and we can bully our way into taking it. These reasons wouldn't work in a human context to override fundamental human rights and they similarly don't work in overriding fundamental rights of animals either, no matter how small the animal might be.

It's challenging to contemplate a shift in perspective and how we live our lives to incorporate an ethical belief with which we might be unfamiliar. Coming to terms with how to reconcile veganism with your life may sometimes seem daunting. All the efforts are worthwhile because they demonstrate a deep commitment to a better world for everyone, from humans to the humble bee. Going vegan is simply powerful.

Chapter 2 Takeaways

- The heroism of veganism is both overstated and under-stated. Although you may not get a cape, it may help you connect more fully all those beliefs in fairness and justice you already hold.
- In a conflict between humans and animals, there are no winners.
- If someone seems receptive to our concerns about animals, the environment or social justice issues, then they may also be receptive to hearing about veganism.
- Many people would've gone vegan sooner if they had understood the moral or ethical implications of veganism. You can go vegan at any age.
- Living a life of non-violence starts with each of us and extends to all sentient beings.
- People go to great lengths in making reproductive choices; yet, we take babies away from other females with impunity.
- Living with non-vegans can be difficult. Sometimes the best you can do is live by example and continue to be approachable.
- Our pets are our companions. Adopt don't shop!

CHAPTER 3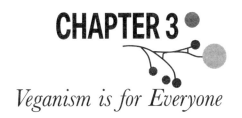

Veganism is for Everyone

Veganism is inextricable from social justice. That aspect is often missing from discussion. How do we begin to change that?

If You Believe in Social Justice, You Believe in Veganism

While in Delhi late one evening, on the drive back to the hotel after a terrific meal in a Kashmiri restaurant, our taxi stops at a traffic light, in the middle of a congested and major intersection. The air is less than salubrious, thick with car exhaust, dust and humidity.

A small, thin child, aged anywhere between five and eight, approaches our car. She's selling balloons. Initially, we think she's a little boy. We can only see a closely cropped head of hair, sweet and sooty face and hands. We can't see the little tattered dress she's wearing. There's an adult nearby who seems to be directing the selling activities, hers and of a few others scattered across the large intersection.

We all fall silent at the sight. We all have the same thoughts; our hearts are shattering and throats constricting. One passenger has leftovers from dinner and she rolls down the window and gives them to her. The little girl happily accepts. She runs off to the median strip between the lanes of traffic and sits down next to an even smaller girl with whom she shares the goodies. As the stop-light and traffic permit, we drive away.

My fellow passengers are some of the most committed people to human rights and social justice issues. They're not vegan and don't consider being vegan is of fundamental importance. This isn't a moral judgment of them. I respect and admire them for their work.

We all see and understand how exploitation affects humans and we're all against it. We understand the arbitrary reasons for this exploitation, whether the reasons are complex or straightforward. None of those reasons are acceptable to any of us on moral grounds. None of us would dream of exploiting humans in the same way.

But when we put animal products on our plates, we *do* behave in a similar way. We don't stop to think about the death and suffering we inflict on completely harmless and vulnerable animals each time we have a meal or a snack. Why? Because we're used to it, we think they taste delicious or they're convenient to our lifestyle. This is analogous to the oppressive and unjust actions by powerful humans upon other humans we can easily read about in history books and see every day in news reports.

The primary reason we use to distinguish our own oppressive and unjust behaviour towards animals is we believe they're somehow *lesser* than us and, therefore, we're better than them. Every reason for this lesser-better judgment on our part is arbitrary because we make up the rules as they're convenient to us in a similar way any oppressor makes them up for their convenience against who they oppress.

During that trip, I had much time to reflect upon this and other similar incidents. Each time, something our friend Ben MacEllen, Australian author, playwright and trans activist, said resonated: 'Every serious and thoughtful social justice activist should, by default, be vegan.'[1]

He's right. How else are we supposed to eradicate a behaviour we find unacceptable if we ourselves are carrying on in a similar way? How can we permanently make the world a more just place for humans when we give little to no justice to beings who are as vulnerable as the little girl selling balloons in traffic? Just as we recognise her right not to be exploited and we fight against social injustice, we must recognise the same basic right for animals and include them in seeking a fairer world for everyone.

Veganism and Poverty: Reconcilable and Intersectional

Whether it's possible to reconcile veganism as a basic moral obligation with the realities of poverty requires that we reflect on the tensions between these two concepts. If these tensions do exist, they're a matter of systemic class and economic oppression – it's not because of any perceived impossibility of understanding the concept of veganism.

When we say veganism is only for the rich, it's important to remember three things. First, animal farming, slaughter and processing industries rely particularly heavily upon poor communities in terms of their location and to supply a workforce. The workforce primarily comprises ethnic minorities, people of colour, migrants, refugees, those with limited educational opportunities and others in vulnerable situations. These industries are generally located in poor communities, ostensibly to bring jobs to communities with limited political clout and long-term economic deprivation. Although they bring some jobs, these industries have a direct negative impact on these communities. Animal agriculture is particularly harmful with respect to, among other things, environmental degradation and resulting ill health, increased mental health issues and domestic violence amongst slaughterhouse workers, worker exploitation because of limited or no other work opportunities and dangerous working conditions.[2]

Exploitation of workers, horrible working conditions, low pay, uncertainty, sexual harassment or violence and the tragic mental and emotional fallout from such experiences are also present in large-scale plant agriculture. Just because we're eating plant-based food, doesn't mean we eliminate suffering and injustice from our diet. We mitigate some of the suffering and exploitation we contribute to, but we can't ignore the plight of farm workers. On the contrary, our eating plant-based food should make us more aware and demand equitable political change for those who plant, grow, pick, pack and distribute our food.[3]

Second, and this may be surprising to some, many people feed themselves primarily with plant-based food because those are the cheapest and most accessible sources of food available.[4] It's the predominantly, but not exclusively, *Western* cultural idea of an adequate diet rendering the consumption of large quantities of animal products as something to aspire to. For some, eating animal foods signals status and wealth. It may be regarded as superior or fashionable to replace traditional, often plant-based foods with animal products.[5] Changes in traditional diets, whether in Europe or elsewhere, to more so-called Western diets come with environmental degradation (see Chapter 6) and lifestyle or food-related diseases (see Chapter 5), such as heart disease, hypertension, Type II diabetes, cancer and stroke, which are now prevalent in many parts of the world.

Third, some poor communities, particularly in the West and often of colour, suffer a much greater proportion of lifestyle or food-related illnesses than rich, often white communities, as a result of limited food choices, lack of access to affordable and healthy food or limited availability of information about healthy eating.[6] In some rich Western countries, poverty can limit access to plant-based foods, fresh or otherwise, which is an outrageous injustice. Put simply, McDonald's can be cheaper than fruits and vegetables. Places where it's difficult or impossible to obtain affordable, nutritious plant-based food are sometimes called food deserts, although some activists prefer the term *food apartheid*.[7] Whether food deserts exist is disputed. For the purposes of this book, we assume they do and it seems to us the term food apartheid is more apt.[8] The issues giving rise to food apartheid are serious and related to class and race.[9]

Therefore, when we're thinking about the tensions between poverty and veganism, the question becomes whether anyone *can* be vegan. The answer is yes.[10] There's nothing stopping someone from understanding the concepts and making the decision to go vegan. Whether someone goes vegan or their efforts to do so are thwarted or hindered because of food apartheid, deprivation, hostile conditions or practical reality are separate matters for everyone to understand, dismantle and remedy. If systemic oppression forces people to make moral choices they don't want to make, then we need to dismantle the system creating the overarching oppression, and provide access to information and solutions inspiring different moral choices, including the choice to go vegan.

Using a human-context analogy, we can substitute the word speciesist and test how another type of bigotry would be reconciled with poverty. In this case, let's use sexism.

- Is sexism always wrong? Yes.
- Do we have an obligation to others not to be sexist? Yes.
- Is it okay for a poor person to be sexist? No.
- Are those subjected to sexism still harmed, whether at the hands of a rich or poor person? Yes.
- Is there something else to explain the sexism other than poverty? Yes, for example: asymmetry of power, traditions, systemic sexism and misogyny or lack of education and opportunities.
- Do any of these reasons give a sexist person a pass to continue being sexist? No, why should they? They can explain the person's mindset. They can help us understand where they're coming from and what, if anything, might be changeable, who might be influenced positively to change, or what might be done.
- Is it easy to discuss or address sexism with a person, whether rich or poor? It may or may not be. We won't know until we do it. For the most part, discussing any issues of fundamental rights can be difficult or, at the very least, a delicate matter, and will require creativity and sensitivity to begin to effect any change. And sometimes, the only thing we can do is say nothing which in itself is a powerful tool.

- Are we judging the person who is being sexist by engaging in a conversation and questioning their behaviour? No, we're not. Although we're not judging them as a person, it doesn't mean we have to like or condone the sexist behaviour or encourage it to continue.

The same logic applies to speciesism. There are myriad reasons to be speciesist, simply because speciesism is the current cultural norm. It doesn't have to be. If anyone can be poor and not sexist, then anyone can be poor and not speciesist. If we have enough respect for women to discuss not being sexist, then we must afford the same respect to animals, and begin to discuss speciesism and veganism with people in the same manner.

The reality is appalling and ghoulish. In vulnerable and exploited segments of our global communities, there's a disproportionately large reliance upon, or access to, food that will ultimately harm the health of those community members and the environment surrounding them. In the same way these communities are vulnerable and exploited, so too are the animals who are the embodiment of that limited food supply. The communities' food becomes a physical representation of their vulnerability, both in terms of human and animal concerns.

Poverty underpins and compounds oppression. Poverty makes everything more difficult, with very little energy left for anything other than how to survive each day. Poverty robs people of reaching their full potential; it is a tremendous drain of their mental and emotional resources. We must dismantle the oppressive structures keeping people poor and making it so easy for animal food to be the *only* available choice; the only affordable choice thanks to subsidies and the power of big business;[11] the only choice because there's no viable transportation system to a market with plant-based food options; the only choice because people are afraid to leave their neighbourhood because of violence stemming from systemic racism and poverty; or the only choice because there's no knowledge of a better choice. We can simultaneously tackle class struggle and poverty and encourage veganism as a moral baseline. These already intersect in many ways. Asserting they can't coexist betrays the animals and belittles people's intellectual abilities.

Animal food production is heavily subsidised by governments all over the world. Big businesses, such as the international fast-food chains, benefit from subsidies with respect to animal food production, animal feed crops such as soybeans, corporate tax breaks and preferential tax treatment; their businesses are set up to make it as cheap as possible to produce, manufacture, distribute and sell their products.

Exploitation and the Patriarchy

How do we expect a society based, at least in part, on the power of a patriarchy to shift the paradigm with respect to exploitation and objectification of women when we can't shift the paradigm in our own daily lives with respect to our own exploitation and objectification of non-human animal females?

The arguments we give for continuing to use, exploit and kill female animals are very similar to those perpetuated to use, exploit and perpetrate all manner of unspeakable violence towards women. 'Such as?' you ask: *We need it. We have always done it this way. Tradition. Religion. Culture. They're not intelligent. They're inferior to us. We have the power and they don't. I don't care. I want what I want. I make my living this way. It's the natural order.*

When we speak of including all our most vulnerable *sisters* in terms of feminism, equality and fairness, we *must* include our non-human animal sisters. They too are vulnerable, like us. They're sentient, like us.

Dairy and eggs are exploitative bodily products produced exclusively by female bodies. In the case of dairy, cows are subjected to continuous cycles of impregnation, gestation, birth and mechanised lactation. To obtain milk, cows must first be forcibly artificially inseminated before giving birth. After birth, their babies are taken away either immediately or within a very short time. Sadly, mother cows vocally mourn for their babies and emit long lowing sounds for extended periods of time. There's no reason to assume other animals don't feel similar levels of pain when we separate them from their children and this is something even Maimonides recognised over 800 years ago.[12]

If born female, a baby cow may follow in her mother's fate. If born male, they're slaughtered for veal or beef. Either way, the calves will never see their mothers again, and for herd animals, such loss and separation is a permanent source of mental and emotional anguish.

In terms of maternal health, the mother cows suffer from mastitis, a very painful condition from which lactating people can also suffer. It's possible for pus from the condition and for other infections to pass into dairy milk. Dairy cows don't get to die of old age on a lush green pasture as the advertisements would have us believe. Once the dairy cows can no longer produce high volumes of milk, they're slaughtered in the same slaughterhouses where cattle bred for beef are also killed. The average lifespan of a dairy cow is four to six years, while their natural lifespan is between fifteen and twenty years. And before we think 'at least the cows had a life', we must consider both the continuous pain in their life and the fact we breed the cows into existence in the first place, just for the purpose of exploiting them.

What's the reason for these conditions? Simply so humans can drink the milk meant to nourish and grow a baby cow. We're the only species feeding on another species' mother's milk, and the only species continuing to consume milk after weaning when there's no longer any nutritional need for that milk.

In the case of eggs, the cycle of exploitation is similar. Egg-laying chickens are selectively bred to lay a huge number of eggs well beyond the capacity and cycles of their fowl cousins in the wild. Once the eggs hatch, we gas or grind up male chicks alive, in a process called maceration, because they're worthless to human use – they can't lay eggs.

For meat consumption, we selectively breed broiler chickens, creating monster-sized beasts so there's more meat to sell and an increase in profit margins. Chickens are slaughtered at mere months of age, when their natural lifespan would be between seven and eight years (see 'A note on ages of farm animals for slaughter compared to natural lifespan' in Chapter 1).

That animals perceive the world differently than we do, or that they look entirely different to us, or that they're less intelligent than us, are irrelevant considerations with respect to their fundamental right to live free from being a commodity. They share this same fundamental right with all humans, just as women deserve the same fundamental human rights as men, regardless of their colour, ethnicity, ability, disability, sexual orientation, size, religion or gender identification.

The dairy and egg industries exploit female animals for their female reproductive systems. They're exploited *because* they're female. This must resonate with us women. Furthermore, these industries – and it's immaterial whether they're industrial or mom and pop farms because only the magnitude of scale changes – are just as deadly and awful as the meat industry.

We must choose veganism for our non-human sisters so our words of inclusion for all women have full meaning. If we can't reject the daily, gruesome exploitation and death of animals and if we can't imagine going vegan because we can't give up a tasty dish, then how do we imagine the patriarchy is ever going to give up their tasty status quo? Why should they?

The Mechanisms of -Isms are the Same

We've decided it's morally and socially acceptable to use, exploit and kill animals because their *not* being like us means we can use them as we please. We believe the trillions of animals we use, particularly for food products, have no purpose other than to be things at our disposal.

THE SORTS OF THINGS WE SAY TO
JUSTIFY USING ANIMALS FOR FOOD AND CLOTHING
Mmm, tasty! Bacon though! Fashion! Tradition! Health! I don't
have time! It's always been this way! God says it's okay! They're
stupid! They're farmed for our use! I don't know how to cook!
We treat them well before we kill them! I don't want to be different! I'm addicted to cheese! It's manly!

Similarly, racists, sexists, ageists, ableists, heterosexists or xeno-
phobes have decided those of us not sufficiently like them
have different or fewer rights than they do. The person can be
denied their basic rights, used, exploited, mistreated, jailed,
tortured, beaten, neglected, cast off, or treated significantly
differently, all for the shallow reasons of not being like the
members of the group who are making those judgments.

We aren't equating human suffering with animal suffering.
We aren't minimising human suffering by making these analogies. We aren't replacing the human suffering and injustice we
wilfully perpetrate on one another with the suffering and
injustice we wilfully perpetrate on animals. We merely recognise all these issues exist simultaneously and stem from similar
roots in our psyche and social systems. Therefore, it's useful to
use our understanding of human injustice and unfairness to
expand our moral circle to include all sentient beings and help
facilitate a deeper level of understanding regarding the impact
and effects of our actions and our choices.

The mechanisms of an -ism are all the same. One group
believes themselves superior to the other. When those notions
of superiority are the norm, it's very easy to believe there's no

problem with acting in line with those norms, even if the suffering of the oppressed group is evident. This mechanism and result apply equally with respect to using animals. Consequently, if we're not vegan, we're demonstrating the same behaviour or thought patterns with respect to animals as someone who believes they're inherently superior to another human. If we're not vegan, we too are saying *we're* inherently superior to *them*. Just as we learn to recognise, and fight against, the misguided notions relating to superiority with respect to other people, we can also learn to do so with respect to animals, and both are essential.

A Vegan Experiment

There are many schemes or challenges to get people to try going vegan, such as a month, week or twenty-one days. We understand the marketing appeal of such schemes and acknowledge they work for some people. Nevertheless, we should consider their implications.

Imagine if someone were to market a similar scheme in connection with not being sexist, ableist, homophobic, classist, ageist or racist? Would any of us say, 'Oh I've signed up for an experiment in not being sexist for three months. There was no reason not to. It's good for my emotional health, I'll feel better about myself, I'll make the world a better place for that time, but, you know, it's so tough to take women seriously.' We can't really imagine that. It would simply be unacceptable socially and morally. We could imagine the scenario if such challenges weren't undertaken as a sort of game and were coupled with serious discussions of the underlying ethical notions of the rights of the group in question, making it explicit the rights continue to exist even after the challenge is over.

Instead, when it comes to animals, we accept all manner of shenanigans. From articles praising journalists who go vegan for a spell of time and tell us about their travails in seitan and tofu, to Meatless Mondays or assorted baby steps. Why does this difference exist? Because we're clear and unambiguous when we talk about anything concerning justice or fairness in a human context. And when we talk about non-human animals, we demonstrate a bias towards speciesism, irrespective of whether we're consciously doing so.

Because we live in a non-vegan world, we're used to putting ourselves above any other species of animals. When it comes to thinking and talking about the issues, it's not surprising we mistakenly frame the issues with ourselves at the centre instead of the correct focus being on the victims who are on our tables. Unlike every other form of exploitation, we pat ourselves on the back for taking a break from it and then go straight back to doing it.

When talking or writing about veganism, some commentators say they don't want to think about what they eat, or go find vegan cheese whilst on holiday, or forever scan labels, or make a nuisance of themselves at dinner parties. What we hear in these complaints is a focus on perceived inconveniences and misconceptions only from the human perspective. Sure, we might have to read labels on packaged food. When we buy a cauliflower, frozen peas or an apple, we're certain there's no reading involved. Or, oh the unimaginable horror, we just don't buy vegan cheese whilst on holiday. None of

these are insurmountable difficulties or particularly complicated additions to our lives.

Most importantly, none of these *inconveniences* make it okay
to exploit and kill animals with abandon. And imagine a guest
saying this at your next affair: 'Oh hey, thanks for the dinner
party invitation. I'm not sexist, but I know you are. So, if you
want to talk rubbish about women, that's fine with me; I won't
say anything because I don't want to be a nuisance! I'll join in
lest you think I'm being a square.'

It's the same with veganism as the outward manifestation of
our not being speciesist. It has nothing to do with purity, being
square, obsessing about food whilst on holiday or otherwise. It
has everything to do with not using animals for our pleasure and
convenience and taking this matter and perspective seriously. If
we thought about the victims of our pleasure, the trillions of
animals who die each year for no good reason, and the very real
human and environmental consequences of animal agriculture,
then it puts these perceived inconveniences in perspective.

Going vegan isn't complicated. We don't need specialised
shops to go vegan, although they're certainly nice to have
around. All we need to do is stop using animals and we've
gone vegan. Simple. There are fresh, frozen or canned vegetables, seeds, grains, beans, fruit and nuts even in corner shops
in small villages and there are supermarkets up and down the
United Kingdom to suit every price point. Even better, that's
the same in most countries.

We don't blame people for being confused or for thinking
veganism is some sort of specialty sport. Some documentaries,
animal groups, celebrities and fashionable animal advocates use
veganism as their own personal theatre to enhance and draw

attention to themselves, just like flagellating monks used to demonstrate their devotion in public during the Middle Ages in Europe. Many of these social channels or platforms don't focus on the unglamorous task of simply and clearly engaging with others. Why? Maybe because this method doesn't provide enough excitement or elicit dramatic emotions from an audience. Many of these channels or platforms never state the simple premise that being vegan is a matter of fundamental fairness and veganism is the least we can do. These aren't complicated concepts and we should be clear about them.

Only Forty-Six Days

The difference between being ethical and being unethical is forty-six days. We know because Farmdrop, a London-based grocery delivery service, tells us so with this advert we saw on the Tube.

How do you like your chicken served: fast or slow?

Supermarkets can grow chicken from a hatchling to shrink-wrapped meal in just 35 days. There's no time machine. They grow chicken this fast by feeding them until they can barely walk, inside mega-sheds where there is no space to roam. The result is a weak, pallid bird with bendy bones and thin skin.

Ditch supermarket fast food with code SLOW for £25 off your first £50 order.

At Farmdrop, as an ethical grocer, we only sell chicken given proper time to grow. 81 days in fact. Slow-grown and well roamed just like the ones your grandparents would've eaten. Tastier because they live longer and happier lives. Richer meat for roasting, and more nutritious bones for broths.

farmdrop

They tell us supermarkets 'grow chicken from a hatchling to shrink-wrapped meal in just 35 days', and Farmdrop, unlike those unethical supermarkets, is 'an *ethical* grocer . . . only sell[ing] chicken given proper time to grow. 81 days in fact.' All it takes for us to be ethical humans is to wait an additional forty-six days before killing a chicken. And according to the ad, they're 'tastier because they live longer and happier lives.' How convenient *for us*!

Imagine if we added forty-six days to the sentence of an innocent death row inmate and we then call their execution ethical because of those extra added forty-six days of life. Should the innocent prisoner be grateful? Should the chicken?

How conveniently we assuage our conscience. If we were writing a more in-depth analysis of this advert, we might point out supermarkets don't *grow* chickens, they're born. In fact, chickens neither moult their feathers nor hurtle themselves on the execution block to then wrap themselves in shrink wrap to be sold as dinner.

Also, if we were writing a more in-depth analysis, we might suggest having extra space to roam for forty-six days doesn't make one deserving of slaughter, particularly when there's no justifiable reason for it.

We might also point out we're supporting the likes of Farmdrop every time we sign petitions demanding governments and companies merely treat animals better whilst they're incarcerated for an additional forty-six days prior to death, instead of being clear the only fair ask is for people to choose veganism. *Better treatment* enables and whitewashes this type of marketing, coddling consumers in thinking their food choices have no ethical repercussions, that they're good consumers because they waited an extra forty-six days and gave the animal 'proper time to grow' before killing them for completely unnecessary consumption. We'd strongly suggest we simply advocate for veganism to make real change.

And we would also mention chickens live for years, not just the *ethical* arbitrary age of eighty-one days, even ones rescued from so-called evil, unethical large factory farms, which are no more evil than our grandparents' farms where death came to all animals in the same way it now comes to them on industrial farms.

But we're not doing any of that. What we're doing is thinking of those forty-six days. That's all it takes for us to wash our hands of any responsibility, fairness or justice we owe animals. Forty-six days. That's all a life is worth. How little for a life.

We're drawn back to 'What Would Be the Answer in a Human Context?' from Chapter 1. Seeing things like this reminds us about what we discussed in that chapter and how key that question really is when thinking about our relationships with animals. Most importantly, though, it really brings to bear the importance of being the approachable vegan so we can have the tough conversations with others and perhaps persuade them to choose veganism too.

Chapter 3 Takeaways

- Rejecting speciesism is analogous to rejecting racism, heterosexism, sexism, ableism, ageism and other forms of oppression because we understand we owe fundamental rights of equality to those who are different to us.
- Feminism must include our non-human animal sisters. The dairy and egg industries exploit female animals for their female reproductive systems.
- The perceived inconvenience of veganism is a trifle compared to the trillions of animals who die each year, and the very real human and environmental consequences of animal agriculture.
- Basic fairness requires we go vegan because focus on improving farm animal treatment doesn't sufficiently challenge the use of animals.
- Better treatment of an animal while in captivity or organic meat doesn't transform killing an animal into an ethical action.

CHAPTER 4

Money and Politics

We examine animal use and exploitation in a global context and consider what the massive new market for vegan or plant-based foods might mean for veganism, humans and the animals. We also look at a few examples of political and legal developments concerning animal laws. Some view these developments as *wins* for the animals. We consider their implications, particularly how much of a victory these really are.

Body Count

We often hear shouts of *victory!* and *progress!* whenever there's a news article about decreased meat consumption, an increase in non-dairy milk or other vegan products for sale, more vegan options at restaurants, an improvement in welfare standards for farmed animals or promises not to use this or that animal for our entertainment. We're told meat reduction campaigns or others similarly encouraging a reduction in consumption of animal foods are successful and beneficial. We're never exactly sure how the success of such campaigns is objectively measured and we're generally sceptical.[1] As such, we use two of our standard questions to evaluate these claims. One is *body count* and the other is *follow the money*.

In law school during the mid-nineties, our criminal law professor[2] taught us *body count*. He would present a fictionalised crime scene and we would count the bodies, whether dead, injured or somehow affected by the criminal actions. Counting the bodies would help us identify the possible crimes committed. In addition, the term was a reference to the heavy metal band from Los Angeles and we're a fan. Body count is helpful here because if the current prevailing advocacy approaches were successful, we should see fewer animal bodies. A decrease in the supply of animal-based foods would be the logical outcome of decreased consumer demand for those products.

Follow the money is a phrase coined in the film *All the President's Men*. The application here is very simple. The data we present will show you where and how people, companies and governments are spending money with respect to animal products. If there were a drop in demand, we'd see less spending and investment on the supply side. We'll also look at changing consumer and business landscapes and what that shows us with respect to animals used as food commodities.

To understand the extent of the global demand and supply of animal products we need to look at data. Below, we present a variety of facts, figures and trends from large markets around the globe, which illustrate the extent of the problem and pervasiveness of animal agriculture both in terms of participation and its economic impact. We also point out where there have been shifts in demand from one animal to others, which have been largely driven by a variety of campaigns to shift or reduce consumption of *meat*.

Worldwide

Research published in 2017 shows the number of land animals slaughtered for meat in 2014 was:[3]

- 62.01 billion chickens
- 1.47 billion pigs
- 648.74 million turkeys
- 545.08 million sheep
- 444.17 million goats
- 300.07 million cattle

These numbers exclude dairy cows and egg-laying chickens because these become other products, food or otherwise, when they're slaughtered. They're not usually destined for meat as such.

Global projections show meat production will 'grow by 17% over the coming decade.'[4] Chicken will make up the bulk of this growth and 'account for over half of the predicted increase in demand – perhaps reflecting the fact that, compared to other meat products, it isn't subject to widespread religious prohibitions – and as a result it will become the world's most consumed meat protein.'[5] Chickens account for 77% of the 30 billion land animals living on farms today.[6] 'Low production costs and lower product prices have contributed to making poultry the meat of choice both for producers and consumers in developing countries.'[7] Further, 'As a global average, per capita meat consumption [excluding fish and seafood] has increased approximately 20 kilograms since 1961; the average person consumed around 43 kilograms of meat in 2014. This increase in per capita meat trends means total meat production has been growing much faster than the rate of population growth.'[8] In short, it doesn't look like people will stop consuming animal products any time soon.

USA

American meat consumption is higher now than it was in the 1970s. Sure, consumption of cows and pigs has decreased, but tell that to the poultry; Americans eat more chickens now than they ever have before.[9]

Despite the reduction in the consumption of beef, the US is still the number one producer in the world[10] (although it's number three in beef exports), and Americans increased their beef consumption by half a pound (227 g) per person in 2015, to 54.3 lbs (25 kg) per person in 2016.[11] In fact, the US is slated for record high red meat and poultry production through 2019[12] and has exceeded the high records for the previous four years,[13] with projections of continued growth in all red meat and poultry categories. Why is that? Because the price of beef has declined due to people demanding and eating more chicken instead of cows. Consumption reduction campaigns don't necessarily lead to veganism. They lead to a shift in demand from cows to chickens.[14]

Ah, bacon! The ever-favourite meat isn't a growth market. Consumption of pig meat is flat in the US, while pig meat production is at an all-time high[15] and pork prices are at an all-time low.[16] The lower price will entice more Americans to eat pork products and it will also make them attractive exports to foreign markets, such as China (depending on the recent trade war, of course).

Surely, we'd expect dairy production to be on the decrease with all those wonderful and delicious new non-dairy milks and cheeses on our shelves! Unfortunately, not so much, despite decreases in liquid dairy milk consumption. The US is the second largest dairy milk producer in the world;[17] according to the US Department of Agriculture, during the third quarter of 2019, the average number of milk cows was 9.32 million.[18] In 2018, there were approximately 9.4 million dairy cows in the US, a number that has increased 2% since 2008.[19] The industry has somewhat recovered from the historic low of 9 million dairy cows in 2004. The numbers are *low* (sobering to think of 9 million per year as a low number) because 'improving technology and genetics have allowed milk output per cow to rise steadily, increasing by 88% since 1980'[20] and an overall 13% increase since 2009.[21] Every year average milk production per cow exceeds the prior year's production and has done so for the past twenty years.[22] In 2019, this figure reached 23,505 lbs (10,662 kg) on average per cow.[23] The strong growth of US milk production over the last forty years corresponds to 'growing domestic and international markets for dairy products, particularly for cheese and various dairy-based food ingredients.'[24] Despite Americans drinking less dairy milk,[25] continued strong production means there's a massive glut of dairy cheese.[26] The production of dairy and dairy cheese is supported by the pervasive system of government subsidies for dairy farms.[27] Sure, those non-dairy products on the shelves are a nice addition to the panoply of consumer offerings. They're tasty and there's some good news there with more and more people normalising plant milks in their diet. But their existence, albeit good, doesn't mean there are significantly fewer cows getting exploited and killed each year.

We can hear you ask us, 'But haven't you heard about all those dairy farms closing? And what about the bankruptcies of the two biggest American private-label dairy milk producers?!' Yes, this is all true. Dairy farms are closing and not simply because people are drinking more non-dairy milk. It's worth exploring a few reasons for the closures: consolidation, change in consumer behaviour and debt levels.

First, large companies have entered this space, consolidating production, lowering point of sale prices and squeezing margins. Large companies can leverage economies of scale, can produce more dairy milk more cheaply, and therefore make more profit than even large private, non-corporate farms (and note, the latter are also heavily subsidised by the state, just as their large corporate counterparts are). For example, in 2018, Walmart, one of the world's largest food and consumer goods retailers, opened its own dairy processing plant in Indiana.[28] The plant supplies own-label milk to hundreds of its stores. The motive for this investment is Walmart will be able to further reduce operating costs and pass those savings on to Walmart customers.[29] Walmart isn't the only American supermarket chain doing this. Kroger and H-E-B, other large supermarket chains in the United States, have already made this switch.[30] If these big companies are getting into the dairy business, it means it's still lucrative to do so.

Second, Americans are drinking less dairy milk and their breakfast choices have shifted away from the classic cold breakfast cereal which would usually be doused in it.[31] Americans have also shifted to consuming more non-dairy milk, with approximately 44% of milk consumers purchasing both dairy and non-dairy milk in 2018–2019.[32] As of October 2019, non-dairy milk sales made up $1.8 billion of the US milk market, while dairy milk made up $12 billion.[33] Both competing forces have eroded fluid dairy milk sales. This is partially good news because plant milks are becoming run of the mill and not some strange or special option.

Third, in late 2019 and early 2020, two of the US's largest and oldest private-label dairy milk producers, Dean Foods and Borden Dairy, filed for bankruptcy protection whilst they attempt to restructure their businesses.[34] For both companies, their biggest customers were the large supermarket chains like Walmart, Kroger and H-E-B, which, as already mentioned, have their own-label dairies.[35] In addition, both companies carried a significant amount of debt, which became increasingly impossible to service, especially as interest rates have risen.[36] These factors aren't unique to Dean Foods and Borden; they've affected and driven into bankruptcy many US dairies.[37] In any event, bankruptcies such as Dean Foods' and Borden's don't mean the dairies are shutting down or ceasing operations. Both companies are continuing operations and exploring a variety of options in reorganising and restructuring their businesses. While there is some good news with respect to the normalisation of plant milks, the dairy industry in the USA is far from being over.

China

In 2016, China introduced new dietary guidelines recommending halving individual meat consumption to between 40g and 75g per person per day.[38] This news seemed encouraging and sent frissons of delight throughout the Veganverse. Public relations firms and celebrities seized on this news and made a video targeting American and Chinese audiences, urging them to reduce their meat consumption for the sake of the planet.[39] Well, reality is rather different. The new Chinese guidelines stem from nice intentions, of course. *Follow the money* and you find a different reality where the meat and animal products industries are actually growing. Reconciling the stated guidelines and the reality is impossible.

China is fourth in global beef production.[40] Sure, the nation seems to be doing something to lower its carbon footprint, but Chinese companies are also investing in all facets of the beef market, whether domestic, overseas, retail or processing.[41] They're doing this because demand for cow meat is rising. No celebrity or dietary guideline will halt the juggernaut, unless there's a shift in the perception and understanding of veganism.

The country is also the world's third largest producer of dairy milk.[42] In 1949, the country had a herd of 120,000 dairy cows. Today, the herd numbers 13 million, and from consuming almost no dairy over the past thirty years, China now consumes 30 kg of dairy products per person per year, with the government recommending people consume three times as much. The aim from the country's central economic plan is to move away from small herds to large industrial ones to meet this demand, which means more exploitation, suffering and death of an ever-increasing number of cows.

The nation is also investing $10.74 billion over the next three years in thirty-five pig farming projects located between its border with Russia to its border with Vietnam. The purpose of these investments is to increase China's pig herd by 25 million.[43] Imports of pig meat are also at record high levels.[44] Pork is shipped from the US (although trade has been in flux as a result of the recent US-China trade war[45] and African Swine Fever afflicting pigs in China[46]) and Europe, with Germany leading those exports.[47] The Chinese government has reserves of both frozen and fresh pork to ensure price stability.[48] Between May and July 2016, to contain a surge in pork prices due to high domestic demand and low supply, the government released over 3 million kilos[49] of frozen pork into the market. In 2019 and in response to African Swine Fever, China is likely to once again use its frozen pork reserves before further increasing its pork exports.[50]

In 2020, China signed the Phase One trade agreement with the USA, which streamlines access to the Chinese meat market for American companies.[51] Under this deal, China will increase its purchase of US beef, pork and poultry products by at least $12.5 billion in 2020 and by $19.5 billion in 2021.[52] China already purchases almost 20% in value of the US exports of 'broiler' chickens.[53] The politics of trade seem to be trumping the intentions of the dietary guidelines.

Alongside increased investment in beef and pork industries, China has increased tenfold its investment in foreign agriculture in less than a decade.[54] What, if anything, this means in terms of food-related economics or geopolitics is a complex subject outside the scope of this book. It's worth pointing out China is doing nothing materially dissimilar to what American or European companies have been doing since the end of the Second World War.

The United Kingdom and Europe

In the UK, '92% of adults eat at least one type of red meat' per month.[55] Despite a slight dip in consumption following the World Health Organisation's finding that red meat is a carcinogen[56] and the higher price of red meat compared to alternatives such as pork or chicken, the industry expects that the sector will 'overcome its short-term difficulties' and that consumers will return to consuming beef.[57] The predicted strength of the British beef market bore true through 2018.[58] During April 2018, the UK produced 77,600 tonnes of beef and veal, which was 13% more than in April 2017.[59] In 2018, there was also a 9% increase from 2017 in prime cattle slaughterings, which excludes dairy cattle, and a 28% increase in slaughterings of adult cattle, including dairy cattle.[60] In 2018, prime cattle slaughter was approximately 1.98 million head.[61]

In 2019, 'approximately 28.8 million farm animals were killed for meat' in the UK, an increase of 5.4% in two years, despite the growth of plant-based diets and products.[62] On average, '78,900 cows, sheep and pigs were killed per day in 2019, up from 74,800 a day in 2017'.[63] Demand for cheap meat drives the increase in industrial-sized pig and poultry farming in the UK from 1,669 in 2017 to 1,786 in 2020.[64] Industrial-sized cow farming, including dairy, isn't monitored for size because such intensive farming doesn't require the same environmental permits as pig and poultry farms, so no numbers are available.[65] From 2018 to 2019, sales of beef dropped in the UK by 1.8% from £3 billion to £2.99 billion.[66] The drop was due to a decrease in the volume of sales and a slight decrease in retail price. Some of the decrease in volume was due to changing consumer demand of the type of meat from roasting joints to mini roasts and healthy mince and shifts in diet to vegetarian, vegan and flexitarian.[67] It was also due to fewer barbecues because of a wet summer.[68] Despite these drops and interesting shifts in demand because of diet change, the numbers still remain incredibly high with 86% of households purchasing beef during 2019, compared to 87% in 2018.[69]

The UK is eating more eggs now than in the last fifty years, consuming approximately 13 billion eggs per year.[70] Retail sales of eggs increased between 3 and 4 per cent in 2019, which was 'their thirteenth year of consecutive growth, the equivalent of 220 [million] more eggs purchased than in 2018.'[71] In part, this is due to more people 'moving towards meat-free regimes – either permanently or occasionally'.[72] Someone might skip having a burger on one day, but it doesn't mean they're any closer to going vegan. People are shifting from one animal food to another.[73] They're making either an incomplete connection or no connection at all between the foods they eat and the injustice they perpetrate on animals. The British egg and poultry industry believe growth in that sector will continue, with higher-welfare chicken schemes and cage-free eggs creating a two-tier pricing system, which will benefit revenue.[74] It's interesting to note the monetary benefit 'humane' farming will bring.

The European Union is the world's third largest producer of beef[75] and consumption of pig meat is stagnant to declining, while pork production is increasing. This seemingly conflicting trend 'suggests that a higher proportion of pig meat is being consumed in foodservice or as processed products, which may fit in better with modern lifestyles. Some may even be used for purposes other than human consumption.'[76] What this means is how much producers profit from these different uses of pig meat is less than how much they would profit if consumers ate pork directly. It doesn't mean fewer pigs are being killed.

India

Unlike what some people believe, just because many in India are vegetarian it doesn't mean India is a cow's paradise. India is the number one dairy milk producing country in the world.[77] It accounts for approximately 19% of the global dairy market share.[78] In addition, the country has been a leading consumer of dairy products since 1998. Many global dairy producers are looking to the Indian consumers to expand their markets with value-added dairy products such as yoghurt and probiotics.[79] As expected, the Indian dairy industry operates no differently than any other dairy industry located elsewhere. In the end, all dairy cows end up in slaughterhouses. As a result of its massive dairy industry, India has many cows to slaughter. What happens to all those carcasses? India is currently the second largest exporter of beef in the world[80] and fifth in beef production.[81] We're sure as many of you are surprised about these statistics as we are.

And as for the idea of India being a cow's paradise, you may have heard about the nation's cow sanctuaries. The investigative work of Yamini Narayanan is essential reading on this topic. She spent years visiting such sanctuaries, called gaushalas in Hindi, located throughout India. Gaushala cows are exploited for dairy and meat just like on commercial dairy farms. 'In 2000, the Delhi High Court uncovered that out of 89,149 bovines that had been sent to the Delhi municipal gosadan (sanctuary for abandoned street, ex-dairy cows), only 8,516 cows remained, with no accounting for the remaining animals . . . In a 2004 case . . . the Madras High Court noted that temple gaushalas were selling cows to slaughterhouses.'[82]

Although beef and pork consumption in India may not be as large as elsewhere, chicken consumption is growing at around 12% a year, making India one of the fastest growing markets in the world for chickens.[83] As we saw earlier, demand for chicken is growing worldwide.

Brazil

Brazil is the world's largest exporter of beef products, although it's second in overall beef production.[84] In 2018, beef exports were the highest ever recorded for Brazil, with Asia being the largest destination, particularly Hong Kong and China, followed by Europe, the United Arab Emirates and Chile.[85] The USA doesn't register in these figures because it banned Brazilian beef imports in 2017.[86]

We'd be remiss if we didn't discuss soya production and its relationship to animal farming and deforestation. Brazil is the world's largest soybean producer and exporter, dwarfing what has historically been a sizeable production in the USA.[87] The US-China trade war started in 2018 has helped Brazil's soy farmers overtake their US counterparts.[88] Soybeans are processed primarily for soy meal, which is the main ingredient in animal feed.[89] Only a very small percentage of cultivated soybeans end up as food for humans.[90] 'About 6% of soybeans grown worldwide are turned directly into food products for human consumption. The rest become animal feed, or are used to make vegetable oil for cooking or for non-food products, such as biodiesel. 70–75% of the world's soy ends up as feed for chickens, pigs, cows, and farmed fish.'[91] So much for those who believe they're avoiding soy if they don't eat it directly or for the notion of tofu and soy milk harming the environment.

The 2019 and 2020 Brazilian forest fires are a continuation of a practice that began over twenty years ago.[92] The overwhelming reason for deforestation is soybean farming, followed, at vastly lower numbers, by sugar, coffee and logging.[93] Although deforestation in the Amazon all but stopped during 2016 to 2017 because there were laws restricting it and agencies monitoring and enforcing those restrictions,[94] since then, deregulation of land and agricultural laws, defunding monitoring and enforcement agencies and other *reforms* have resulted in a resurgence of the practice.[95] Deforestation isn't only occurring in the Amazon. It's also in the Cerrado, another ecologically important area of Brazil.[96] Deforestation creates additional pastures for cattle and arable land on which to cultivate the soybeans for animal feed all over the world.[97] This further underscores why advocating for meat reduction is insufficient.

Obviously, deforestation also affects and kills wild animals. Moreover, this practice has always been and continues to be a land grab, displacing and killing indigenous people.[98] And we all know how deforestation contributes significantly to the increase in global levels of carbon dioxide that will affect all humans.[99] Once again, animal agriculture isn't only about our concern for the animals, but for the very real and deadly effects on humans. There's no avoiding that.

Where do we go from here?

Unfortunately for the animals and people, we're far from winning or even truly progressing in reducing either demand for animal foods or the supply of animal bodies. Although there have been some shifts, generally current wisdom in animal advocacy promotes reducing consumption instead of simply advocating for veganism. The standard arguments seem to be focused on how we treat animals – their *welfare* and *humane* animal use – with little to no simultaneous challenge to speciesist notions regarding the *use* of animals. In short, we're overly concerned with *how* we use animals and not sufficiently discussing whether we should be using them at all.

Basic fairness requires we go vegan, but instead the world is living in the vain hope a baby-steps approach will, in an indeterminate future, convert people to stop using animals. Without a shift in our dialogue clarifying that veganism is an essential element of a just and fair society, the animals will continue to die by the trillions.

Some people blame capitalism for the massive consumption of animal products and there is, of course, truth to that. Humans have been farming animals for at least 10,000 years, through a variety of economic systems. Capitalism is only a magnifier for our well-established behaviours and proclivities. It's our demand for animal products that's driving the business, capitalist or otherwise, of using and killing animals. Discussions about whether to dismantle capitalism are important, no doubt. We can't have any economic or political discussion without also addressing our demand for animal products.

We're sorry for bringing such stark facts to the fore. We need to understand the reality so we may build and tell a new story – a vegan story. We know the world won't go vegan overnight. It might never if we're not clear veganism is our necessary goal because it's quite evident neither better conditions for these animals before they're killed, nor a reduction in the amount of meat we're eating will be enough.

Despite the overwhelming data that might make us feel powerless, we can do something.

Every day we're vegan we're doing something towards that goal. If we want to do more, we can, and it doesn't have to be complicated. We can engage with people who may be interested in veganism. We can use our skills, talents or hobbies to share the basic concepts we talk about in this book, and practical things too, such as cooking, meal prep, shopping for food and other advice. We can use events or news stories as springboards for simple conversations; even new vegan products can be a good start. We can organise with others to conduct a variety of educational activities, whether on a small or large scale. There are limitless ways in which we can be activists.

In any conversation or activity, we can always be clear about what we want for the animals: freedom from exploitation as objects. Simultaneously, we can and should be our best selves when we interact with non-vegans. Let's remember this: despite rising numbers of vegans, there really aren't that many of us in comparison to the overwhelmingly non-vegan majority. People need to see us, get to know us and understand what we want. If we send mixed messages, how will we get to that?

WHAT WOULD WE DO IN A HUMAN CONTEXT?
Imagine, for example, the suffragettes. They educated women and men around them about recognising the right to vote for (some) women. Also imagine those who fought for workers' rights, gay rights or civil rights. They all educated those around them about why it was necessary to recognise the rights inherent in each group. None of their ideas were instantly popular with the majority, but eventually, discourse, minds and society changed.

Beyond Meat

Vegan products are no longer only the purview of specialty shops. By 2025, the global vegan food market is expected to be worth US$24.06 billion.[100] The UK is setting the pace for this growth with a market worth £310 million and more new vegan products launched in 2018 than in any other country.[101] In 2019, over a quarter of all new food products in the UK were labelled vegan and growth of meat-free foods grew 40% to £816 million.[102] And in the USA, over 40% of Americans have tried plant-based meats and six out of ten would eat them again.[103]

The first significant investment by a public company in plant-based food took place in the USA in 2016 when Beyond Meat was a vegan start-up, manufacturing burgers and sausages made from a unique combination of peas and beans, and getting ready to make a massive splash. In October of that year, Tyson Foods invested in Beyond Meat. Tyson is an enormous company. Their sales in 2019 were over $42 billion.[104] Tyson is the American market-leading 'multi-national, protein-focused food company', producing '1 in 5 pounds of all chicken, beef and pork in the U.S.' and providing protein to 'restaurant chains, including quick service, casual, midscale and fine dining restaurants . . . to schools, military bases, hospitals, nursing homes, international customers . . . club stores, grocery stores and discount stores.'[105] It's also the only company in the US selling 'chicken, beef, pork and prepared foods products through all major retail distribution channels.'[106] Tyson's choice of words to describe its products, *protein*, is notable and disconcerting in their reducing sentient creatures to mere biochemical molecules.

At the time of Tyson's investment, the Veganverse bubbled over with excitement. The world didn't go vegan overnight, despite effusive social media updates. Anecdotally, we saw many social media posts exclaiming Tyson Foods' investment was an admission of its fear of vegan power or Beyond being a threat to Tyson's market for meat. We don't believe Tyson feared vegan meats. We believe it saw a great opportunity to make money in this new and developing sector of meatless and meat-replacement foods, and to maybe learn a thing or two for this potential new market.

In 2016, Beyond Meat was a small, privately held company. Right from their start, Beyond was often in the news. Their product distribution in the US grew tremendously (well, to go from zero to anything above that is going to be tremendous growth) and everyone agreed it had further space for market penetration. In addition, Beyond took all the risk of developing and creating a new product and marketing it to vegans and non-vegans alike. All these factors made Beyond an interesting investment for Tyson because there was potential for financial gain.

Fast forward to 2019, Beyond becomes a publicly traded company. The initial public offering (IPO) documents include a variety of financial information from which we can see the size of Tyson's investment, approximately $8 million.[107] That figure might have been lower in 2016 and increased over time. We've no way to verify this theory. At IPO, Tyson had 731,301 shares of publicly traded stock, which was approximately 6% of Beyond, and at $25 per share, which was the IPO price, Tyson had an investment worth approximately $18.3 million.

For the relatively small sum paid in 2016, Tyson put a teeny tiny bet on a potential winner. They diversified their investment portfolio, which is something companies like to do, especially when it comes at such a small price. To illustrate, compare the magnitudes of the $8 million investment to the enormous $7.7 billion merger in 2014 between Tyson and Hillshire Brands, a food-service company. And to further illustrate diversification, during its involvement with Beyond, Tyson realised there was potential in the market for plant-based meat and announced its own line, Raised & Rooted.[108]

The growth of Beyond Meat is an overall positive. It's good to have more plant-based food choices readily available for purchase. It's good to hear discussions about plant-based foods on national and international news. But Tyson has nothing to fear from the surge in demand for plant-based products, vegans or from Beyond. In fact, and somewhat confoundingly, Tyson recently introduced a product mixing pea protein with animal products, such as their Angus beef and pea protein patties.[109]

The consumer market for plant foods, particularly packaged and prepared foods, is growing, and we'll see more stories like Beyond's. This growth is an expansion of consumer choice. But the existence of plant-based food products is neither evidence of fewer animals dying nor proof there's a wholesale public shift in thinking about using and consuming animals (see 'Body Count' in this chapter for some evidence).

The existence of these products is evidence of how capitalism works. It's up to us to leverage these consumer opportunities into conversations with others about why we shouldn't be using and consuming animals in the first place. If we can have those conversations over a tasty Beyond product, then so much the better.

A Wicked Good Opportunity

Tesco is a very large publicly traded food retailer in Europe and parts of Asia. In 2018, Bloomberg reported the introduction of vegan ranges was at least partially responsible for improving Tesco's finances,[110] and since that time, Tesco has greatly expanded its range of vegan products and ready meals. This is good news in many respects. Before we get our party hats on, let's put this news in context and examine what Tesco's new products mean and what opportunities they create for vegans.

As we've discussed before, having lots of vegan consumer choices doesn't mean a vegan world is here or will ever come. It doesn't mean fewer animals are dying. It doesn't even necessarily mean Tesco understands or cares about veganism. Tesco is a corporate entity beholden to its shareholders like any other corporate entity and it has the vision to let the talented vegan chefs of Wicked Healthy do their thing: develop plant-based ready meals and convenience foods for Tesco shoppers. This is fantastic because we need culinary vision and tasty vegan food in as many places as possible.

In its crudest form, Tesco's food range expansion means capitalism is functioning as always, by providing consumers with more products and creating markets to generate and increase revenue streams and profits. In a more nuanced form, financially viable vegan options available in the mainstream means vegan businesses will be taken seriously when they seek financing to set up or expand. It also means a market for vegan food isn't just in its infancy, relegated to urbanite or hipster outposts. It has begun in earnest. Many other supermarkets have followed Tesco's lead, introducing and expanding vegan product lines. Now, companies and the public will have a better sense of what vegans eat.

These changes in the food market have at least two potential outcomes: 1) they normalise vegan food, and 2) vegan food is no longer the sole purview of specialised shops. Convenience, packaged or prepared plant-based foods, including sweets, cheeses and milks, are now on shelves in many conventional supermarkets, sometimes alongside similar non-vegan products.

Vegan food becomes ordinary when people see these new products with the word vegan or plant-based (or, often, both) printed on them on supermarket shelves. The mystique or perceived strangeness of vegan food dissipates, making it easier for people to visualise and access vegan foods and see for themselves being vegan isn't difficult. However, new products might not dispel the myth that being vegan is expensive. Sometimes, specialised, prepared or packaged vegan products may be more expensive than non-vegan products, as we discuss in 'Frugal Vegan' in Chapter 5, although this too is changing dramatically.

Most importantly, the existence of these products creates new opportunities for a variety of conversations, including: questioning and challenging ourselves and others to rethink habits and assumptions; examining the disconnect between loving animals and killing them; and showing the only thing that matters in terms of the fundamental similarities between humans and animals is our sentience, and our differences in skin, size, intelligence and abilities shouldn't be a death warrant or carte blanche for exploitation.

These conversations with our family, friends, neighbours or strangers in a supermarket aisle can change the world.

What About 'No-Kill' Eggs?

There's a new advancement in agricultural science called, rather vividly, *no-kill* eggs.[111] As always with these supposedly humane advancements, the alleged reduction of harm doesn't mean there's not continued needless exploitation or a death sentence awaiting the animals involved in the whole process.

In the case of no-kill eggs, male chicks won't be slaughtered simply because they'll never be born, which is undoubtedly a very good thing. Nothing changes for the females, who will continue relentlessly laying eggs until they're routinely slaughtered as soon as their egg production diminishes. The resulting eggs are only *no-kill* because of the *absence* of male births, not because *no* animal dies.

Also, as is always the case, the reason for these advancements isn't a sense of fairness: they're driven by economics. Humane advancements ease consumer squeamishness over the notion of killing live chicks in grinders or by asphyxiation – in other words, they make us feel better about our food choices, produce eggs more cheaply and for a higher profit, and continue to sell the products of animal exploitation.

The no-kill technique involves scanning eggs by laser and air pressure nine days after they've been fertilised to determine their sex. If the egg would develop into a male chick, it's disposed of before it's born. This admittedly very ingenious process avoids having to destroy 4 to 6 billion male chicks born and slaughtered annually in global hatcheries. They're slaughtered because they're *useless* to the egg industry. They can't be sold either alive or dead.

Nothing at all changes for their mothers and sisters. They're exploited throughout their lives. They're killed because they're female. They produce a product we desire and have no *need* to consume. Our desires, apparently, trump their lives.

Some herald this technique as a step forward in compassionate animal agriculture. Practically, it's only a measure to increase profitability while continuing to exploit female bodies until they're spent. The point is that no-kill eggs fall into the same category of entrepreneurship as some of the examples in the rest of this chapter: the innovation is driven by profits, not ethics. Sure, the hatchery will no longer have the image problem with, and running expense of, disposing of the dead male chicks. Instead, it will create a premium product for which they can charge more. The hatchery will likely be able to use the increasingly vapid term *sustainable* to influence consumers to purchase its more expensive eggs. Neither compassion nor fairness is relevant here, because if either were, then the only answer would be to stop consuming chickens and eggs.

There's a less addressed issue wrapped up in this too. Many of us, vegan or not, focus on whether an animal is treated well, including killed humanely. On the one hand, we don't want animals to be treated poorly; on the other, we'll accept they'll eventually be killed for food. What a contradiction!

Campaigning for incremental better treatment of animals ignores the source of the problem. Some examples of incremental better treatment are how male chicks are killed; allowing baby cows to stay with their mums for an hour or a day before being permanently removed so the mum can provide milk for humans; and larger crates or cages or enriched environments for the mental stimulation of animals. Focusing on better treatment instead of whether *using an animal at all* is morally justified, creates a confused narrative. You can imagine a non-vegan asking, 'What more do you want? You've got the no-kill eggs, larger crates, humanely raised or free range. Now let me eat my *humane* omelette, steak or bacon.' The focus on treatment suggests it's okay to own and use animals for our benefit so long as it's done humanely or we treat them well before we kill them. There's simply no such thing as humane meat.

Whether vegans support the implementation of humane measures is immaterial. They'll happen with or without us. We're not driving those changes. Financial gain is the driving force. Businesses will of their own volition undertake whatever is cheaper or more profitable for them, including implementing all the humane or compassionate reforms in animal agriculture (see 'Size Doesn't Matter' and 'The California Fur 'Ban': What Does It Actually Accomplish?' in this chapter). They'll implement those reforms because it helps their bottom line. Instead, let's think about what message are we sending when we celebrate or commend a restaurant chain when they commit to using only eggs from free-range chickens or exclusively selling organic meats, a pig farm when it transitions to housing their sows in larger cages, a fashion house when they decide to forego fur or leather and they continue to use wool, or an aquarium when they agree to no longer use one species for entertainment and they continue to use other species? While we recognise there are incremental benefits to the day-to-day lives of those animals involved, in all these cases, the underlying and needless exploitation and death continue, maybe not for one or the other animal, but for all the rest. Instead of celebrating, might we leverage those moments as conversation starters? For example, if a friend is happy about free-range eggs or large crates for sows, then they might be open to a conversation about the concepts underpinning veganism we discuss in this book.

REPRODUCTIVE SYSTEM THOUGHT EXPERIMENT

In the case of eggs and dairy and analogising those to a human context, would anyone accept as ethical any technique, no matter how humane, justifying continued exploitation of women as objects solely for their reproductive system?

When it comes to responding to these issues, the animals have no voice. Of course animals resist, attempt to escape and demonstrate their suffering, but they can't hear how we negotiate with their lives; and, most importantly, they can't object using our language. We shouldn't discount their fundamental rights just to appease the non-vegan majority in the mistaken belief this majority will someday wake up to the truth. No animal, human or non, is an object to be treated as economic property and we've no right to use them as such.

Size Doesn't Matter

There are many types of initiatives where we try to diminish animal suffering through legislation. For example, the proposed ban by France and Germany on culling male chicks born as *by-products* of the egg-laying industry.[112] Although these initiatives share the goal of reducing some suffering in the *treatment* of animals, none address or engage with the fundamental question of whether we should be *using* animals in the first place. Stopping the use of animals will also stop issues over treatment. The reverse isn't true.

In 2016, Massachusetts voted on a ballot initiative on whether 'to prohibit the sale of eggs, veal or pork of a farm animal confined in spaces that prevent the animal from lying down, standing up, extending its limbs or turning around.'[113] If the question were 'Is it necessary to kill animals for humans to live happy, delicious and healthy lives?' then this ballot measure would be something to get excited about. What's less exciting is a ballot initiative over what the size of the cage must be for us to deem it humane enough to allow us to buy animal products. The outcome of the ballot doesn't change the fact animals will die.

With respect to Massachusetts' chickens, all farms but one already used larger cages and, allegedly, there were no farms using crates for baby cows or pigs.[114] Businesses in the state came up with these practices on their own, without any legal obligation, because before the 2016 vote there were no explicit prohibitions against small cages or enclosures. Massachusetts agribusinesses had already adopted this gilded-cage model, following national and international trends and practices, which started in 2007.[115] The odds of established businesses reverting to obsolete practices are slim to none. Why would they? So why did they need to outlaw something that was already *not* happening?

Some advocates praised these improved animal welfare models because they improved the lives of these animals to some extent. But there was little public discussion about the ultimate fate of the animals, regardless of how they were treated within their lifetime. In any event, the industry was already moving to improved welfare standards on its own. What these advocates were seeking not only already existed, but it supported the status quo for animals. In addition, proponents of the ballot measure also claimed the effect of the prohibition on the sale of animal products from animals raised in small cages would force other states wanting to trade with Massachusetts to upgrade to gilded cages as well. Eventually, the thought was, all US states would follow.

As for the detractors, their only concern was that eggs from higher welfare hens would become more expensive. They claimed eggs were 'a nutritious staple food used disproportionately by low-income families' and 'most nutrition advice now favours greater egg consumption, especially for consumers who cannot afford more costly sources of high-quality protein.'[116] The claim about the change in nutrition advice about eggs is mistaken. Most nutritional advice doesn't favour consuming more animal products, eggs or otherwise.[117]

In addition, the detractors' *concern* over the diets of low-income families is disingenuous. As we discussed in Chapter 3, low-income families in the USA shoulder a much greater burden of diet-related, chronic diseases than the population as a whole and, for a variety of reasons, they also don't consume enough fruits, vegetables and healthy grains.[118] Therefore, there's no basis upon which to continue to peddle the pernicious myth of the necessity or superiority of animal protein when science and nutrition tell us otherwise. A much more worthwhile discussion would be an analysis of prices and overall availability of pulses, grains, fruits and vegetables for low-income residents of the state, and what, if anything, is being done to ensure everyone has access to, and can afford, such beneficial foods.

Both the concern over price and the concern over the size of a cage failed to consider one important thing. Whatever the monetary value of the animal product or the size of the cage, the animal who produces the secretion or whose body parts make up the products we buy, pays the most valuable price: their life. Non-vegans and non-activists wouldn't readily make this connection. It seems even some activists fail to do so.

The Humane Society of the United States (HSUS) was heavily involved at the time of the ballot and since. Paul Shapiro, the HSUS vice president at the time of the vote, said, 'There have to be some rules with regard to our conduct towards those who can't defend themselves . . . You're talking about a cost that's extremely modest by any account with regard to not keeping animals locked in tiny cages.'[119] If the aim was to defend those who can't defend themselves then why support larger cages? They're accepting half-measures, which are unacceptable to us. The cage won't defend them from continued exploitation and slaughter.

Also confusing was a statement on the matter by Matt Bershadker, president and chief executive of the American Society for the Prevention of Cruelty to Animals at an event at the Massachusetts State House. He said, 'This measure asserts that society will no longer accept the abject suffering of animals as a pathway to profit.'[120] Is killing not the *ultimate* abject suffering? And Melissa Ghareeb, former barn manager of MSPCA at Nevins Farm, said, 'It is unconscionable to cram animals into cages so small they cannot turn around or extend their limbs.'[121] Of course it's horrific. Is it conscionable, then, to kill them at all, even if they've lived marginally better lives? What have the animals done to require such extreme retribution from one's conscience? She also goes on to say, 'Voters can stop cruelty in its tracks, by voting yes.' Voting is a civic duty we discharge every so often, while eating is something we do every day. It's a lot simpler and more direct to stop cruelty in its tracks by simply choosing veganism.

The measure passed by a wide margin and it's scheduled to go into effect in 2022. Too bad for all those unhappy chickens on the sole Massachusetts farm using too small cages from now until then, but a win is a win. Or is it?

Since the vote, Massachusetts was obligated to fend off lawsuits from thirteen other states who argued the new standard would abrogate their right to free trade. Eventually those states lost, which means the law will come into effect as scheduled. Or will it? Despite the vote, the Massachusetts legislature is proposing changes to the law to bring it in line with laws existing in other states. A proposal they're considering, backed and written by HSUS and the New England Brown Egg Council, reduces the confinement requirements from the voter-approved 1.5 square-feet per bird to only 1 square foot with *enhancements* 'aimed at improving the welfare of egg-laying hens that supply the state's retail market.'[122] This type of system has already been adopted by the United Egg Producers and incorporated into new laws restricting cage confinement in California, Rhode Island, Oregon and Washington.

The irony is the Massachusetts Farm Bureau Federation opposes these new changes. They think advocates should honour the will of the voters, despite their original opposition to the ballot initiative! The Federation's support isn't surprising since all but one farm in Massachusetts was already in compliance. The further question to consider is the role of HSUS. Their supporting these new changes seems like an own goal or bidding against themselves in the ballot initiative they campaigned for and won.

Since the ballot initiative started in 2018, with the court case and other legislative wrangling, people supported the campaign by donating over $2.7 million.[123] HSUS contributed the overwhelming majority. In 2016, Wayne Pacelle, the then-president of HSUS, said businesses were desperately attempting to defeat the ballot measure and it was their last stand against ending 'extreme confinement'.[124] He also said, 'They'll be hard pressed to withstand the influence and reach of our coalition and devoted advocates who toiled to gather the signatures to put this measure before voters.'

It turns out the battle wasn't and hasn't been so desperate. How do we know this? *Follow the money*, of course. The opposition raised and spent just under $303,000.[125] That's how desperate this fight was *not*. Was it not a colossal waste of resources, public energy and enthusiasm to get a measure passed where nothing meaningful really changed? If you had devotedly toiled to get this measure passed, might you be demanding your money and time back? Might that $2.7 million have been used to fund ways to better educate the people of Massachusetts about veganism?

Obviously, we abhor the entire practice of caging animals, whatever the size of the cage. Also, we're not indifferent to the present suffering of animals. It's ghastly. We're asking whether it's time well spent advocating for gilded cages in the hope someday the existence of these cages will convince people to end the slaughter of completely innocent animals. Remember, animal welfare laws and organisations aren't new. The world's first animal welfare laws and organisation were adopted and founded in Great Britain. In 1822, the British Parliament passed the Cruel Treatment of Cattle Act, and the Protection of Animals Act in 1911. The Society for the Prevention of Cruelty to Animals, or SPCA, was founded in 1824. Over the last 200 years these organisations and efforts have existed, our use and slaughter of animals hasn't abated. We've had a lot of time patching together welfare measures, and we're still not asking the fundamental questions of why, and what justifies animal use.[126] In short, our historical and existing attempts to protect animals simply aren't close to enough, and veganism presents the only realistic method by which we can end the exploitation of animals.

We've seen in 'Body Count' in this chapter there's been no reduction in the number of animals killed for food despite all the animal protection, humane farming measures and initiatives we've created. It would be remarkable to see campaigns regularly and prominently incorporate veganism into their message. Such campaigns could be a new and galvanising force. They would educate a wide variety of people who are already concerned about animals and encourage them to choose veganism. If we want to end the senseless slaughter of animals, we need more vegans, not more gilded cages.

> ### SALARY RAISE THOUGHT EXPERIMENT
>
> In a human context, think about it like this: if we want a pay rise but never ask for one directly, and instead only vaguely ask to be treated better, more kindly, to get a better chair and a cute pencil sharpener, we'll never see an additional cent. If all devoted advocates had spent their resources educating and organising themselves around ethical veganism, their efforts may have yielded the results they, in their hearts, genuinely want: to end the suffering and death of animals.

The California Fur Ban: What Does it Actually Accomplish?

In October 2019, following similar bans in Los Angeles,[127] West Hollywood, Berkeley and San Francisco, California banned the manufacture and sale of *some* fur and skins.[128] On 1 January 2023, it will become illegal to manufacture for sale, sell, trade or display any item made from the fur of any animal *except* cats, dogs, deer, sheep or goats. There's also no prohibition on any 'animal skin or part thereof that is to be converted into leather, which in processing will have the hair, fleece or fur fibre completely removed'. Resale of existing or used furs is permitted. Also permitted is the manufacture and sale of fur for religious or traditional tribal, cultural or spiritual purposes by Native Americans.

Californians will still be able to purchase, and have shipped to them, fur from banned animals outside California. They'll be able to wear whatever fur they wish for their personal use. And fur will continue to be manufactured outside California, whether in the USA or elsewhere. Little changes for the animals. The banned fur animals will still be bred, trapped, exploited and killed, no matter how humanely. And the same fate will continue to await all the other animals who didn't make the banned list and who are used for their bodily products.

Despite some fashion houses foregoing fur and some large shops deciding no longer to carry fur, the industry remains buoyant.[129] Nothing has changed fundamentally. Brands and large stores can simply change their minds, like British department store House of Fraser recently did, deciding to carry fur again after a decade without it.[130]

In terms of enforcement, we question how effective the implementation of such a ban will be. Presumably, any enforcement process will begin only after receiving a complaint by the public. There won't be any inspections like those carried out under health and safety laws like there are in restaurants, for example. Violations will be treated as misdemeanours only and not incur criminal penalties. Those who break the ban will only face a civil action of up to $500 for the first violation, $750 for a second violation that occurs within one year of the previous, or up to $1,000 for a violation occurring within one year of a second or subsequent violation. The one bit of teeth this law might have is with respect to any action brought consequently; the costs associated with investigation, attorney's fees and expert witness fees may also be recovered.[131] And it will be tough to reach this point.

Who wins in this fur ban? As usual, it's people who win here, *not* the animals. Consumers who don't wish to see fur in shops might see less or none of it. The large animal groups may claim a win and use it to fuel fundraising activities in other locations to obtain similar hollow results. The state assembly members and senators approved the measures by a wide margin and are seen to have done something good and popular with people without any personal cost to them or any great sacrifice in state revenue.[132] With this 'ban' everyone can signal their moral superiority without themselves having made any changes in their lives to help animals.

When the city of Los Angeles was debating their own ban, Council member Koretz, one of the proponents, made a terrific and impassioned speech:

> Skinning a sentient being is not a practice that can be described as anything other than cruel. I don't think letting the market decide is a solution. We could apply that to human trafficking and say sure we'll let it go on as long as there are people that want to have sex with trafficked people. But I don't think the market is appropriate to decide. And certainly, if you ask the animals, which we don't have a good way to do, they would all tell you they don't want to be skinned alive for their fur. But I think we have to take an action as their voices. The voices of the voiceless.[133]

He's right, and his reasoning applies to all animals.

Let's look at an example of how markets decide. In 2018, storm Florence hit South Carolina. The death toll for farm animals was approximately 5,000 pigs and 3.4 million chickens and turkeys out of a total 9 million pigs and 819 million fowl populating agribusinesses across the state.[134] Insurance pay-outs on those 'losses' were based on calculating the market value of those lives. The lives of those sentient beings were valued only as the objects they represented, akin to a lost car or mobile phone. When we consider Councillor Koretz's words in context when he said we shouldn't let the market decide whether a sentient being lives or dies, that's exactly what we do every day when we choose *not* to be vegan.

What makes fur worthy of special consideration as opposed to banning any other textile made from hair, feathers, hide or secretions of an animal? Our fixation with fur goes back almost a century. The first fur protests were held in the USA in the 1920s against trapping practices.[135] Here we are a century later and fur is *still* here. While we're so focused on fur, leather and wool get a free pass for no decent reason.

'Wow, you've bummed me out,' we hear you say. 'Is there any hope?' Of course there is! These bans are amazing opportunities. They bring up great questions to help us think about the issues surrounding veganism and they allow us to examine our reactions and get our thoughts straight. We can then seize these moments when people are thinking about the needless suffering and death of animals and have conversations with our friends, families and communities to help them connect the dots to their daily eating habits. Bottom line: we need them to go vegan if we're truly going to make real and meaningful changes for *all* animals.

Chapter 4 Takeaways

- Global demand for, and supply of, animal-based products are expected to continue to increase for the foreseeable future. To drive these numbers down, we need more vegans.
- Campaigns to reduce the consumption of meat don't necessarily result in people going vegan. They'll often just shift to eating other types of animal products.
- Every day we're vegan, we're doing something to promote veganism. If we can do more, we might start by engaging others about the basic concepts of veganism.
- More vegan products on supermarket shelves is neither evidence of fewer animals dying nor proof there's a public shift in thinking about using and consuming animals. However, the growing plant-based food market normalises vegan food and can help us start conversations about why we don't need to consume animal products in the first place.
- If we want to end the senseless slaughter of animals, we need more vegans, not more laws.
- There's no morally relevant difference between leather, wool, feathers, silk and fur.

CHAPTER 5

Healthy and Frugal Vegan

We deconstruct some of the myths of veganism being a cure-all or an expensive food trend. We also compile excerpts from well-respected medical and nutritional institutions about a vegan diet and health.

What the Experts Say

Well-respected medical and dietary institutions agree that being vegan is healthy at any stage in life. The list below, complete with the relevant passages quoted from those institutions, is an indispensable resource.

Academy of Nutrition and Dietetics[1]

Appropriately planned vegetarian diets, including total vegetarian or vegan diets, are healthful, nutritionally adequate, and may provide health benefits in the prevention and treatment of certain diseases. Well-planned vegetarian diets are appropriate for individuals during all stages of the life cycle, including pregnancy, lactation, infancy, childhood and adolescence, and for athletes.

British Dietetic Association[2]

Well-planned plant-based and vegan diets can support healthy living at every age and life stage.

Dietitians Association of Australia[3]

Vegan diets are a type of vegetarian diet where only plant-based foods are eaten. With planning, those following a vegan diet can cover all their nutrient bases.

Dietitians of Canada[4]

Anyone can follow a vegan diet – from children to teens to older adults. It's even healthy for pregnant or nursing mothers. A well-planned vegan diet is high in fibre, vitamins and anti-oxidants. Plus, it's low in saturated fat and cholesterol. This healthy combination helps protect against chronic diseases. Vegans have lower rates of heart disease, diabetes and certain types of cancer than non-vegans. Vegans also have lower blood pressure levels than both meat-eaters and vegetarians and are less likely to be overweight.

Cleveland Clinic[5]

Eating a plant-based vegetarian or vegan diet can be a healthy, exciting alternative to traditional meat-based meal planning. Obtaining proper nutrients from non-animal sources is simple for the modern herbivore. There is a wide variety of vegetarian/vegan-friendly meat/dairy/egg replacements currently on the market. Recipes are abundant on the Internet as well as in a variety of vegetarian cookbooks.

There really are no disadvantages to a herbivorous diet! A plant-based diet has many health benefits, including lowering the risk for heart disease, hypertension, Type 2 diabetes and cancer. It can also help lower cholesterol and blood pressure levels, plus maintain weight and bone health.

Harvard Health Publishing – Harvard Medical School[6]

Nowadays, plant-based eating is recognised as not only nutritionally sufficient, but also as a way to reduce the risk for many chronic illnesses.

Mayo Clinic[7]

Vegetarian diets [including vegan] continue to increase in popularity. Reasons for following a vegetarian diet are varied but include health benefits, such as reducing your risk of heart disease, diabetes and some cancers.

Yet some vegetarians rely too heavily on processed foods, which can be high in calories, sugar, fat and sodium. And they may not eat enough fruits, vegetables, whole grains and calcium-rich foods, thus missing out on the nutrients they provide.

However, with a little planning a vegetarian diet can meet the needs of people of all ages, including children, teenagers and pregnant or breast-feeding women. The key is to be aware of your nutritional needs so that you plan a diet that meets them.

National Health Service (NHS)[8]

With good planning and an understanding of what makes up a healthy, balanced vegan diet, you can get all the nutrients your body needs.

NutritionFacts.org[9]

These are the top fifteen reasons Americans die [prematurely], and a plant-based diet can help prevent nearly all of them . . . can help treat more than half of them, and in some cases even reverse the progression of disease, including our top three killers.

Veganism as a Measure of Health

We had friends who would tease they could spot vegans by their blue-tinged skin tones, thinning hair, and the way their bones stuck out at their ribs and hips. These misconceptions were fuelled by the way society, and big business, frames anyone who dares not to participate in animal exploitation.

A quick internet search of 'is eating vegan healthy' will bring up article after article defending the role of animal products in proper brain function, or the necessity of animal proteins for physical fitness, or how B12 deficiencies are equivalent to a diagnosis of early death (we exaggerate, obviously). As time passes, we've noticed a shift in the stereotype. As science continues to work on backing up plant-based diets, people are forced to find more creative ways to counter the positive findings. What used to be an argument about protein and eating enough calories is now more commonly focused on a *safe* quantity of carbs, how *natural* supplementation is, and whether cooked or raw produce is more important for optimal health. The thing is, with a vegan diet being vastly different from one person to another, just as any non-vegan's diet is vastly different from another's, it's incredibly speculative to pigeonhole all vegans as having one set of advantages or disadvantages over other lifestyles and dietary choices. Doing so sets people up to fail because they'll never be able to fulfil others' expectations of how vegans should be, look and function, instead of highlighting our shared moral choices. And imagine the confusion we create when people hear conflicting extreme points of view, one saying vegans are the most unwell and the other saying they're the fittest.

In comparing vegan and non-vegan diets, vegans are also often expected to not just live a balanced life but to exceed the nutritional requirements of any diet it's compared to. And in those comparisons, disease prevention takes a back seat to the hyped-up aesthetic benefits of cutting back on animal products. The expectation is for vegans to be simultaneously like athletes, nutritionists and health practitioners. Through diet alone, vegans are expected to overcome any predisposition to body type or physical abilities when we know diet isn't the only measure of health. We want people to understand going vegan isn't something we should encourage solely for health or physical gains, as these aren't *guaranteed* results. Vegans share the common goals of removing violence from our lives and replacing it with fairness towards animals. Understanding these goals means veganism becomes inclusive of everyone irrespective of age, physical ability, size or chronic illness. We can be ill or healthy irrespective of being vegan.

Despite all the serious medical and dietary institutions supporting veganism and its benefits, people's understanding of what vegans eat isn't becoming any clearer. Sure, people are hearing you *can* live without meat and dairy, but these same institutions aren't showing them *how*. When people following traditional food pyramids, paleo plans and other meat-centric diets make the decision to be vegan, the switch may appear to them to have an animal-based protein hole.

To fill the hole, people swap meats with tofu, tempeh or prepared faux meat products. The misconception is there's a protein deficiency in a vegan diet, which fuels the misguided argument for how unhealthy being vegan can be. No one claims vegans need any more or less protein, carbohydrates or fibre than non-vegans. We're constantly measured, and our diets scrutinised, by whether we can *surpass* non-vegans with our eating habits, not on how we fare nutritionally.

Are all non-vegans inherently eating balanced diets? No. Are all vegans inherently eating unbalanced diets? Also no. Rather than measuring the worth of a vegan diet based solely on how similarly it can mimic a non-vegan one, people ought to remain focused on why they're choosing to eat vegan in the first place. Only then can vegans better appreciate the impact of their diet not only on themselves, but also on the world around them.

Some of the benefits of going vegan are now public knowledge, with lower risks of cancer[10] and heart disease[11] being commonly celebrated discoveries across many studies. Nevertheless, we've noticed for every social media post on the dangers of loading up on bacon, there's one celebrating the promise of clear skin, stamina or the loss of those 'last 10 lbs' by eating vegan. Besides the obvious benefits of getting more greens in your diet, people claim you'll look younger, find definition in your abs, and some even go as far as saying you won't experience gas, stomach aches or bloating, all of which are absurd claims. Plants alone can't cure what's 'wrong' with us, especially those superficial flaws we're told we need to fix.

Look, we couldn't be more pleased with the results people have when they eliminate animal products, or the fact more people are seeing these reasons as ways into lifelong veganism and not just a plant-based diet. Promoting these unrealistic standards as absolute results of following a vegan diet doesn't help either the current vegans, who are expected to live up to a false standard, or the animals, when it should be all about them in the first place. There are many other factors than the foods we eat, or the weight we carry, when talking about the subjective qualifications for what entails health.

Have you noticed how vegans are the only people expected to drop nutritional information at a moment's notice? We've somehow become the model for health, when the diet aspect merely focuses on the exclusion of animal products, and not the specific inclusion of anything else. As the popularity of plant-based athletes and celebrities rises, more misinformation is being published by way of meal plans, recommended daily amounts of supplements and before-and-after shots. It's a really good idea to learn the requirements for your body to thrive, but that's not done online, or at the recommendation of someone you've never met. Where we all unite is in the elimination of another's unnecessary suffering, not in the pursuit of finding our abs or living to 100 with flawless skin.

With ethical veganism at the helm of our motives, giving up animal products was easy. Considering the well-being of animals also made the difficult work of educating ourselves about our own needs, cooking and healthy living habits that much easier. Although your social media feed might say otherwise, you don't have to eat avocados to be vegan. Likewise, you might not reach a goal BMI, lessen the symptoms of an illness, or suddenly sprout mermaid-length hair. That's okay, because choosing veganism is about choosing fairness and non-violence towards animals. This choice must also extend to compassion for ourselves, and knowing when a claim is just a stereotype. We might look up to vegans who have forged a path of wellness for us or we might choose to eat our weight in vegan cheese. Being vegan isn't about eating better or being better than your neighbour, it's about doing everything we can as individuals to fight to end animal exploitation. Our choice to be vegan is for the benefit of animals first.

Disordered Eating in Veganism

Our concerned parents, co-workers and the confused masses often worry veganism is nothing but a low-cal, low-energy, bird food diet. There's a false stereotype of all vegans sustaining themselves on celery sticks, but we're part of a wave of vegan mac 'n' cheese aficionados who are constantly challenging what it means to eat vegan.

A persistent misunderstanding is that veganism can facilitate disordered eating in some vulnerable people. Disordered eating exists everywhere, at dinner tables with menus spanning cultures, generations and a multitude of diets. As we've said, nothing is guaranteed by going vegan. The variety, complexity and completeness of how a vegan eats are, like for anyone else, down to the individual.

Turning to a plant-based diet to forego food or restrict our caloric intake isn't participating in the non-violence of veganism. Veganism is a way of life, not a diet.

In veganism there's no portion requirements – you can eat what you want when you want, and everyone is different, with different body shapes and sizes. We remain individuals with individual needs. Fad 21-day diets and juice fasts often pose as what's normal for vegans to eat, but they're not. Health experts and professionals know enough about nutrition today that they should be able to help vegans vulnerable to disordered eating just as they help anyone else with the same conditions. It's important to take care of and nurture ourselves and we *can* do so without sacrificing the lives of others. If we're looking to place blame for disordered eating, the pressure to look a certain way is certainly not limited to veganism.

Vegans may know the ins and outs of which bugs are used to create which colours of candy,[12] but our aversion to specific foods isn't only about what they'll do to our bodies, but what supporting the creation of that item means for all animals involved in its production. Whether we suffer from disordered eating is a separate and important matter. We have the power to help people live well on plant foods and that should be part of the focus of our veganism.

Frugal Vegan

If our idea of vegan food means shopping at Whole Foods, eating exclusively organic, and only dining at popular, hipster vegan restaurants, we might be correct in assuming avoiding animal products is costly. With no real consensus on what represents an average diet, there are boundless variables that might inflate the cost of a shopping list or dinner bill. With so much emphasis on faux meat, vegan cheese and non-dairy products to show the simplicity of substituting their non-vegan counterparts, very little is being done on a large scale to educate people on the necessity of choosing healthy, whole, and in this case, cheaper foods. While a store-bought vegan deli meat might make a faster or easier sandwich, it's not necessarily going to make the cheapest or most sustainable swap in the longer term. Vegans who've made the switch and hope to keep it may want to be better versed in methods for eating more frugally.

If a non-vegan were to rhyme off their weekly meal plan and it included lobster, filet mignon and caviar, there would be little opposition to the suggestion that choosing veganism would be less costly. But you see, when it comes to measuring the cost of beans, grains and vegetables against meat, cheese and dairy, there's no comparison. In a large supermarket, dry beans are only £1.75 per kilogram, and lentils, just over £2 per kilogram.[13] If we compare this to the £2 to £35 per kilogram a variety of meats would cost, you could be eating more beans and lentils for the same price, or the same amount for a smaller price.

People only make the 'isn't vegan food expensive?' argument when they feel the need to substitute their standard non-vegan favourites with a vegan prepared or packaged food alternative. A diet consisting completely of substitute foods isn't necessarily unaffordable, but it might not make being vegan a money-saving measure.

Price differentials between non-vegan and vegan food are most evident when we compare the latter to meat and dairy counterparts which all benefit from government subsidies and huge volume in manufacture and sale. Generally, dairy cheese and meats are less expensive than their vegan counterparts which receive no subsidies and are produced and sold in much smaller volume. Instead, when we compare high quality products, whether or not vegan, made in small batches, the difference in consumer price narrows to some extent.

For example, in 2020, the least costly dairy cheese slices available in Tesco cost £2.95 per kilogram, while the least costly vegan counterpart costs £12.50 per kilo.[14] That's a significant difference, but not when compared to Tesco's priciest dairy cheese slices, which they sell for £12.67 per kilo.[15] If we look at soft cheeses, Tesco sells its most costly camembert at £10 per kilo, while a vegan one, which is artisanal and unavailable in Tesco, costs £50 per kilogram, which is closer in price to an artisanal French dairy cheese, which comes in at £37 per kilo.[16] As for meat products, Tesco own-brand pork sausages cost £1.77 per kilo, while the least costly vegan counterpart costs £5.80 per kilogram.[17] Again, that's quite a difference, although smaller than the difference between dairy and vegan cheese. When we compare the most costly sausages available in Tesco, they sell for £8.83 per kilo, while the vegan counterpart comes in at £25 per kilogram, which is closer in price to gourmet pork sausages priced at £24 per kilo or the fillet steak at £35.56 per kilogram.[18] As demand for vegan products increases, more vegan products will come to market as we've seen in 'Beyond Meat' in Chapter 4, volumes will increase and these price differences will begin to narrow even further. And let's remember, vegan cheeses, burgers, sausages or any faux meat can be easily produced at home, unlike their non-vegan counterparts.

Similarly, misaligned price comparisons also occur where people compare organic produce and prepared or packaged foods to their non-organic counterparts. While many vegans might choose to eat organic for both health and environmental benefits, doing so isn't a necessary component of being vegan, and is something commonly misunderstood and misrepresented. In the case of many grocery store items, packaged or organic items can sell at a higher cost because of people's association with the word *organic*. A bag of organic, vegan and gluten-free cookies might be calling your name, but their sheer existence doesn't by any means make them a dietary necessity. In truth, whole foods that aren't prepared or packaged are naturally vegan and we should be more concerned about them, especially if they don't have a label. Where possible, growing our own food, bulk buying wholefood ingredients and buying plant-based foods from local markets are some of the ways we can meet our desire for better quality foods without compromising our budgets.

A family of four, who rely upon a single source of income and who want to transition to veganism, may want to centre their transition on a wholefoods diet. The emphasis shouldn't be on buying and consuming veganised food. There's a fine line between supporting vegan brands and making it seem as though a vegan life without them isn't worth living. To be told, or to believe, you'll be hungry, unsatisfied, or malnourished without them is also untrue.

Consider a chilli, stew or noodle soup. Someone who eats animal products might make a giant pot with animal protein scraps and homemade animal-based broth. Will the non-vegan dish automatically be more expensive than the vegan alternative? Well, it depends. Were someone to make a pot of vegan chilli with canned beans and vegetable broth, replacing the meat a non-vegan would use with two popular vegan meat replacements such as seitan or tempeh, it could cost just as much to make this vegan chilli as a non-vegan version. Were a vegan to take cost-cutting measures such as soaking dried beans and making homemade stock from food waste, they'd have found the vegan recipe (pun intended) for penny-pinching. Books like *Eat Vegan on $4 a Day*[19] can be helpful tools for mastering cheap, homemade staples. Or if we don't have a lot of time to cook, we could roast vegetables in the oven or cook canned or frozen vegetables on the hob and be done in twenty minutes. Then round things off with some canned beans, a quick grain of whatever type we like, add some seasoning and we're done.

Okay, now that we understand there are ways to eat cheaply and ways to splurge regardless of what diet we follow, why do we forget this in restaurants? Much of the cost of a plate we're served when dining out includes labour, equipment, insurance, taxes and rent, not just the food.[20] While some see paying £9 for a vegetable-based burger as *so expensive* compared to paying only £3 for a Big Mac, consider again the circumstance in which the raw material came to be, and who is serving it to you. A non-vegan burger at a sit-down restaurant would also cost upwards of £8.[21] Corporations running fast-food chains can charge less than a mom-and-pop vegan or non-vegan café that prides itself on making everything from scratch. Fast-food companies benefit from highly subsidised animal products, they operate on very large scales and receive a variety of other tax incentives. These factors have huge impacts on lowering the manufacturing and selling costs and enable corporates to charge lower retail prices while maintaining sizeable profit margins. In addition, we think the reason the restaurant misconception exists is because vegan fast food isn't something widely profitable just yet. Places like Evolution,[22] a vegan fast-food, drive-thru restaurant in

California, are looking to change things with US$6 or US$7 offerings and Beyond Meat are slated to launch vegan burgers at McDonald's and Nando's in the UK.[23]

Just as we use faux meats for dishes we remember enjoying, dining out in vegan eateries is popular for replicating experiences we had as non-vegans. We prefer to dine somewhere making or serving speciality foods we're not about to attempt, or shell out for, at home. We can't afford large bags of maca, a so-called super food. We can afford to add it to a take-out smoothie for a dollar, on occasion.

Another important thing to consider when shopping for vegan staples is serving sizes. For example, a bag of quinoa might seem expensive at £8.75 for 2 kg (thank you, Costco). With one dry cup of quinoa yielding three cooked cups of nutritious protein, one bag will provide approximately eleven servings. When you can look objectively at costs like that, and consider a bowl of quinoa can cost you 79p, it no longer feels as utterly unreasonable to buy the wholesale bag as our gut reaction made it seem. The same can be applied to that £8 wheel of cashew cheese,[24] so long as you don't devour it all in one sitting (good luck). From personal experience, we spend approximately £45 (CAD$75) a week to feed three square meals and a snack to two hungry vegans. That ends up being £90 (CAD$150) a month each, less than some people spend on a single night out.

There's a wealth of information already available to those looking to cut costs in the kitchen.[25] Bulk shopping, coupon clipping, cooking more, and getting comfortable with eating lots of leftovers, are all ways vegans can feel a financial gain alongside their ethical one. Initially, learning to eat well without breaking the bank takes time, effort, and at least a little bit of mental math. When animals are our reason for choosing not to participate in exploitation and violence, choosing plant-based foods over animal products is easy and finding sustainable financial practices for eating in and dining out will follow and become easy hacks and habits. When anyone tries to argue you're spending so much more on food because you're choosing the vegan option, you can always fall back on the incredible 13p price tag on a pound of bananas, better known as vegan gold.

Zoonotic Diseases: Our Deal with the Devil

Zoonotic diseases are caused by germs spreading between animals and people.[26] There are a variety of zoonotic diseases, from rare and obscure ones to those familiar to many of us. Examples of the familiar ones are measles, tuberculosis and smallpox, which all have their origins in pathogens affecting cattle. All types of flu originate in pathogens affecting pigs, ducks and chickens. Pertussis, also known as whooping cough, originates in pathogens affecting pigs and dogs. Malaria has its origins in pathogens affecting birds, possibly chickens and ducks.[27] These examples of zoonotic diseases are some of those whose spread reached pandemic proportions through close contact between people and animals on farms.

We're not here to discuss the COVID-19 pandemic directly. We're here to discuss how our using animals as commodities facilitates diseases jumping from animals to humans, because 'almost half of the zoonotic diseases that have emerged in humans since 1940 resulted from changes in land use . . . or wildlife hunting'.[28] COVID-19 is just one of the most recent zoonotic pandemics. As you can see from our examples, there have been many throughout history.

We don't often think about the farmyard origins of those familiar diseases, such as measles, smallpox, whooping cough, malaria or the flu.[29] We rationalise their existence as just an unfortunate part of life. We accept them as inevitable because we've accepted animal agriculture as something inevitable. We face each new zoonotic disease related to a farm animal and any resulting pandemic as a risk we can't avoid – although we could if we didn't use animals.

We even distract ourselves from the seriousness of some of those diseases, such as measles and whooping cough, by referring to them as *childhood* diseases, as if they were an innocuous rite of passage. They're childhood diseases because they're so infectious; we contract them (or are vaccinated against them) early on before surviving to adulthood.[30] Adults who haven't been exposed or inoculated by vaccine can also contract these diseases, with potentially very serious consequences.

The pathogen cross-overs related to these known diseases had their origins in the familiar farmed animals we still consume today. Diseases such as flu, measles, tuberculosis, pertussis, smallpox and malaria originated in small farms, which were the norm since we began domesticating and herding animals thousands of years ago, until the advent of industrial farming. Some of these diseases wiped out entire indigenous populations, both accidentally and maliciously, and pandemics associated with many of them caused cataclysmic suffering and death all over the world. Most of these diseases continue to exist and kill millions.

Today, in addition to farmed-animal origins, some pathogens are emerging from *wild* animals. For example, HIV/Aids is thought to have originated in chimps through consumption of bush meat.[31] Whether COVID-19 is conclusively traced to a market trading in wild animals will be something science will need to establish. For us non-scientists, it doesn't matter what the species of the animal hosting the original pathogen was, or the location of the initial infection. These are facts useful only for learning more about the disease. It's not relevant to us whether the location of possible infection is a *wet* market in China or a *quaint* farmers' market in Provence or the Cotswolds. These distinctions in types of market are about how some people perceive other cultures and deem some exotic or *dangerous*. Wet markets can be found everywhere, not just in China, and many food and farmers' markets elsewhere also sell animals, alive or dead. They're simply not called wet markets. It also doesn't matter whether the location is an industrial or a small farm, a regulated fish or meat market, a dairy or egg farm, an abattoir or any other establishment breeding, processing or selling animal products. Each of these locations is, and has been, a potential breeding ground for zoonotic diseases and starting points for pandemics. None of these things matter in our thinking about the root causes of zoonotic diseases because our continued use of animals as commodities will always result in novel diseases.

We're all in some way complicit in facilitating the existence of these new diseases, or variations of the old ones. How? There are broadly two categories of reasons. First and at the core, we continue to exploit animals and create the conditions by which these diseases spread to humans. Animal agriculture brings us into close contact with animals in an unnatural and crowded environment. Demand for animal products exacerbates deforestation and environmental degradation as we discuss in Chapter 6, which brings animals and pathogens out of forests and into close contact with people.[32] There's also antibiotic use in animal agriculture increasing antibiotic resistance in people, which will make it impossible or very difficult to treat disease.[33] Therefore, as demand for animal products continues to increase (as we've seen in 'Body Count' in Chapter 4), these factors won't go away. They'll only diminish as more people stop demanding animal foods by choosing veganism.

Second, we're indirectly complicit as citizens of a world whose global economic systems drive us to turn everything, including wild animals, into a commodity at ever increasing speeds. Whether by necessity because there are no other viable means to make a living or by simple greed, people search inexorably for new things to exploit and profit from. This relentless drive to find new products to sell also means more wild animals or other forest products eventually make it to markets in ever increasing quantities. Even if these animals and products were traditionally used by people, the speed and quantities by which they come to market has increased the likelihood of pathogens crossing over. As evolutionary biologist Rob Wallace notes, 'Production cycles degrade ecosystemic resilience to disease as natural resources are transformed into commodities, complicate epidemiological interventions by treating humans and animals as markets and commodities first, and globalize the transport of goods, people, livestock and pathogens . . . capitalist production does not *have* an epidemiology so much as it *is* an epidemiology.'[31]

What's the solution to such indirect complicity? We must strive for an economic system that looks after people, animals and all of nature through international solidarity, demanding a fair production process with equitable sharing of profits, and fair wages and living conditions for all people. We can create solutions if we organise the political will to do so.

The historical argument of having to exploit animals for food, transportation and labour which has permitted humanity to develop as it has done is immaterial *now*. We can't change our past and how we evolved to this point. We used other animals to further our own development. We don't need to continue to do so. Exploiting animals was, and continues to be, a deal with the devil costing human and animal lives.

It's time we upend the old rules, reframe our thinking and advocate for veganism on a large scale for everyone's benefit.

Chapter 5 Takeaways

- Well-respected medical and dietary institutions agree being vegan is healthy at any stage in life.
- Being vegan is neither a guarantee of health nor of illness. It's an ethical choice, not a magic bullet.
- Our use of animals is directly responsible for zoonotic diseases, whatever the location or species.
- You can be frugal and vegan.

CHAPTER 6

Environment

A brief overview of some of the most serious studies linking animal agriculture to climate breakdown. We also look at a strange argument about land use efficiency and question the disconnect between the concern over climate breakdown and being non-vegan.

Environmental Science

At least since 2006, there have been a series of serious studies showing animal agriculture being responsible for an enormous amount of damage to the environment and people. The numbers and methodology of apportioning, and accounting for, total greenhouse gases is a relatively new science, thus the numbers vary and some are controversial. All are worth reading for yourself. We're not here to give more or less weight to any of them. However, the deep and inextricable connection between animal agriculture and environmental degradation and climate breakdown is undeniable.

In 2006, the Food and Agriculture Organization of the United Nations (FAO) found animal agriculture caused 18% of total global greenhouse gases.[1] Three years later, in 2009, the Worldwatch Institute published a markedly different and controversial report. They had audited the FAO results and showed they were grossly undercalculated. They pointed out the FAO report underrepresented the inputs that must be considered to present a complete picture. Instead of 18%, the Worldwatch study found greenhouse gases from animal agriculture accounted for 51% of worldwide emissions.[2] In 2010 the authors of the Worldwatch report, Jeff Anhang and Robert Goodland, were criticised. They've never wavered from their conclusions and have defended their research point by point.[3] Other commentators have also defended their research.[4] Subsequently, FAO published a report, which lowered the original calculation to 14.5%.[5] Despite these significant discrepancies, FAO has nevertheless continued to underscore the role of animal agriculture on environmental degradation and climate breakdown.[6]

Between 2015 and 2019, a variety of other studies were published, further cementing the connection between animal agriculture and climate change and the necessity for humans to switch to a plant-based diet. In 2015, Johns Hopkins University found that if global trends in meat and dairy intake continue, global mean temperature rise will, by 2050, more than likely exceed the target 2°C above pre-industrial levels, even with dramatic emissions reductions and carbon management strategies in place across non-agricultural sectors.[7] In addition, immediate and substantial reductions in wasted food and meat and dairy intake, particularly ruminant meat (e.g., beef and lamb), are imperative to mitigating catastrophic climate change, yet the urgency of these interventions isn't represented in the current negotiations for climate change mitigation. In short, whatever other measures we take to reduce climate change, a large-scale switch to plant-based diets is imperative for our future survival.

In 2018, *Nature* published an Oxford University study advocating for us to switch to plant-based foods to avoid catastrophe.[8] Also, the journal *Science* published a study which found animal products provide 37% of protein and 18% of calories, while being responsible for using 83% of global farmland and 56–58% of food-related emissions.[9] That study also found that a global dietary shift to a completely animal-free diet would reduce food-related greenhouse gases by approximately 49% and the amount of farmland required to feed all humans by approximately 76%. In addition, the study revealed shifting diets away from all animal products in the US, where per capita meat consumption is three times the world average, could reduce food emissions by 61–73%. Simply put, going vegan helps in significantly reducing emissions and increasing efficient use of land.

In 2019, *The Lancet* published two studies and both further established the one basic and irrefutable notion: animal agriculture is killing us and the planet as we know it; and we must shift to eating plants, if we want a liveable future on earth.[10]

These studies and reports have made their way into the public sphere. In 2019, during a lecture at the University of Chicago, Steven Chu, former United States Energy Secretary, a Nobel Prize winning physicist and president of the American Association for the Advancement of Science, said:

If cattle and dairy cows were a country, they would have more greenhouse gas emissions than the entire EU 28 . . . agriculture and land use generates more greenhouse gas emissions than power generation.[11]

While much of the focus may be on greenhouse gases, the negative impacts of animal agriculture aren't limited to those. They include deforestation, displacement of native and indigenous peoples, diseases, antibiotics resistance in humans, animal species extinction, water pollution, human conflict over resources, desertification, acidification of oceans and soil, oceanic dead zones caused by fertiliser and animal faeces, vast amounts of plastic in the ocean due to fishing, soil erosion, flooding, and depletion of water resources.

It's important to note that none of these studies or reports encourage being *vegan*. Instead they all urge to *drastically* reduce consumption of animal foods to a couple of ounces per person, per week. The reasons for such a recommendation, instead of a clear statement to be vegan, are likely tied up with politics, farm and agriculture lobbies, inherent speciesism and animal rights very rarely being discussed in terms of a moral obligation from people to animals. Nevertheless, our moral obligations to those communities on the front lines of climate breakdown clearly intersect with our moral obligations to animals. And even if not everyone shares our belief in our moral obligation to animals, we have moral obligations to people which, in this context, we can begin to discharge at a minimum by simply changing what we eat. We're all on this planet together, and as the least of earth's creatures go, we go. Therefore, discussing one must include discussing the other. Climate breakdown will affect each of us no matter where we are. Whatever the number may be, animal agriculture is a significant contributor to the dark realities we face and no study disputes that. Anhang and Goodland published a response to the criticisms they received, the conclusion of which is as concise and pithy as we're likely to see anywhere:

> While governments continue to struggle to agree on measures that would increase renewable energy infrastructure significantly, we propose that alternatives to livestock products could be scaled up quickly to reduce today's grave risk of climate

change significantly. Indeed, reducing animal feed production and replacing at least one quarter of today's livestock products with substitutes could be the only way for governments, industry and the general public collaboratively to take a single, powerful action to reduce climate change quickly.[12]

The science is clear: animal agriculture has had a variety of devastating effects. If more of us were to take the single and powerful decision to choose veganism and collaborate with others so they too could make the switch, we could have a powerful tool to demand swifter and more decisive actions from our governments to avert climate catastrophe.

Land Use

Sometimes we hear people say how much more land we'd need to feed a vegan world, which is incorrect. Growing plants to feed humans takes significantly fewer resources than our current non-vegan system does. Currently, we grow plants primarily to feed animals. Then those animals are slaughtered to feed humans. This is the inefficient system, not the other way around. Needing fewer resources to feed people plants seems like a straightforward proposition. So, it's surprising when critics misinterpret or misuse land use studies. For example in 2016, a study examined carrying capacity and land use efficiency of ten different diets in the United States, including vegan and non-vegan diets.[13]

A few data points may be helpful to remember before we look at the carrying capacity study. Animal products use 83%

of global farmland whilst providing only 18% of calories,[14] as discussed in the previous essay, 'Environmental Science'. Billions of animals are slaughtered annually. All those animals were herbivores, which means we grow enough plant food each year to feed all of them, even if we consider some might have grazed on land unsuitable for agriculture. 'Livestock is the world's largest user of land resources, with grazing land and cropland dedicated to the production of feed representing almost 80% of all agricultural land. Feed crops are grown in one-third of total cropland, while the total land area occupied by pasture is equivalent to 26% of the ice-free terrestrial surface.'[15] Additionally, 'Grazing animals supply about 10 percent of the world's production of beef and about 30 percent of the world's production of sheep and goat meat.'[16] If we can feed that staggering number of animals each year on the amount of land we have and which provides only *18%* of calories, then we can surely figure out a way to feed plant-based foods to the current estimated human population of 7.7 billion, too.[17]

It's important to recognise the 'estimated 100 million people in arid areas, and probably a similar number in other zones, [for whom] grazing livestock is the only possible source of livelihood.'[18] But it's equally important to recognise the existential threats which environmental degradation and climate change pose to those livelihoods, alongside the increased risks of human conflict arising because of such threats.[19] We can't consider one without the other.

Refocusing our attention to the carrying capacity study, its sole purpose was to determine the efficiency of land use in the US, within the framework of currently existing farming methods and the recommended American diet. The ten differing diets used in the study were the test variables. Land use efficiency was defined as how many people can be fed on any diet on the available agricultural land. The arguably unique part about this study was that the authors partitioned the land into 'grazing land, cultivated cropland, and perennial cropland'.

The carrying capacity study didn't look at water availability or use in different farming methods, health or environmental concerns stemming from agricultural practices, carbon dioxide or methane emissions, or any other fallout from animal farming. The study also didn't consider any ethical obligations we owe to animals, or even to humans. The diets themselves are problematic because we don't believe most Americans are following the study's *recommended* diet in the first place. If they were, the food-related health problems we know exist in the US and in many other parts of the world wouldn't be so prevalent or severe. Therefore, when the authors of the study concluded a vegan diet would decrease land use efficiency, but efficiency would increase if meat consumption were reduced by only 13%, what exactly did this percentage represent, and where does it leave us? Nothing and nowhere, respectively, as demonstrated by the substantial evidence presented in the reports and studies cited earlier in this chapter.

Thus, within this misguided and limited analysis, the study concluded a vegan diet would use land less efficiently than other diets because grazing land couldn't be used to grow crops. This seems circular to us. Sure, grazing land might be unsuitable for food production, but other types of, and spaces for, farming plants would become a reality. For example, land currently cultivated with animal feed crops could be converted instead to the cultivation of crops to feed humans. But it isn't the goal of the carrying capacity study to examine any of this.

On a related note, let's stop and ponder the concept of efficiency itself. Only some parts of nature *might* be based upon efficiency, for example calorie consumption vis-à-vis physical activity, although this is nevertheless an imperfect analogy because nothing is that linear. And even if there were some immutable scientific law about efficiency, we make exceptions for it in our society because we balance efficiency with fairness, or at least we strive to do so.

EFFICIENCY THOUGHT EXPERIMENT

Consider whether it's efficient in an economy for people to have the liberty to move freely between jobs. Why, for efficiency's sake, should anyone get paid to work, or have the right to vote, speak or think freely, learn to read and write or even be free from discrimination? Are these things *efficient*, and if so, in what context?

In the example above, none of these things are *efficient* in terms of producing goods and services, just as grazing land may not be efficient for growing plant crops. We acknowledge all these things are good and necessary, and we adjust society to account for such good and necessary things. Modern society strives to balance efficiency, at least with respect to the fundamental rights of people.

Only part of being vegan has anything to do with health and the environment. The primary focus of veganism is the rights we owe to those beings whom we kill and exploit for nothing more than our habits. This is no more a matter of being efficient, sanctimonious, pure or idealistic than supporting the fundamental rights of others in another context. The efficiency of land use is important and it must be balanced against the rights of others, including animals. When we know the dire consequences of animal agriculture and have enough land to grow crops that would feed humanity, it's disingenuous to use the repurposing of grazing land as an excuse against veganism.

Are We So Different from Climate Change Deniers?

If we still consume animal products knowing animal agriculture contributes more to greenhouse gases than anything else, knowing about its impact upon environmental degradation, deforestation and unbelievable human exploitation, how different are we from those who deny climate breakdown?

Considering the consequences of our actions and not only the language we use, the simple answer is we're not very different at all.

We justify our views on consuming animal products using different language and excuses than a climate sceptic would use. But our actions contribute to it just the same. All our reasons for continuing to be non-vegan are arbitrary and self-serving. In other words, we like keeping things as they are.

If more of us were vegan, we wouldn't need to wait for the government or large corporations to do something – *anything*.

We'd be making the single biggest difference to shift the current impasse and it's the only one over which we have a tremendous amount of personal control because eating is a *daily* activity. We could bring about real change from the bottom up. We could peacefully force a change upon governments and corporations who, otherwise, have a vested interest in keeping things *exactly* as they are.

Meaningful change doesn't only come from above. It can be led by popular shifts in beliefs, opinion, culture and demands. Once these shifts occur, governments and corporations follow suit, implementing changes on a large scale reflecting those popular shifts. And without a doubt, large-scale implementation of mitigating measures is critical to tackling climate breakdown. Large scale, top-down change and new laws come about only once there's support from a broad and vocal enough segment of the population.

Pouring scorn on climate change sceptics or deniers while oneself isn't vegan is nothing more than another excuse, another distraction, from making meaningful changes in one's life. And what's utterly confounding is many people have skin in this game once they have children. At this rate, what are we leaving for them? Don't we owe them a minimum too in terms of doing the most we can to ensure they have a liveable environment?

Veganism is for everyone, whether people or animals. We have a variety of great reasons to choose veganism, from the ethical aspects which underpin it, to social justice concerns, facilitating improving human health and radically affecting the trajectory of the climate crisis, all while eating delicious foods. Changing habits can be challenging and what better encouragement to do so when there's so much at stake.

Chapter 6 Takeaways

- There have been a series of serious studies showing animal agriculture is responsible for an enormous amount of damage to the planet and people. Adopting a vegan diet is a singularly effective and relatively simple measure we can take to begin to make a difference in halting and reversing the damage.
- We have the land required to feed the world on a plant-based diet.
- More vegans mean less demand for animal products and more pressure on governments and businesses to change their approach to farming and feeding the world.
- Veganism is good for everyone – people and animals.

CHAPTER 7

Bringing It All Together

When someone asks 'Why go vegan?' we can't just hand them this book or a flyer and hope for the best. Similarly, when we need to figure out how the underlying ethics of veganism might influence our decision making, we also need something practical. In both instances, we need to be able to think and communicate our reasons quickly, clearly, reasonably, possibly without too much emotion, and make decisions relatively swiftly. Below are short summaries of the broad concepts presented in this book. These summaries are a framework for thinking like a vegan. They'll help organise your thoughts about the multifaceted implications of veganism in all aspects of life. We also propose an *elevator pitch* answer and we hope you find it's a helpful starting point.

1. **Justice** – The basic fairness principle is to accord the same moral treatment to everyone, unless there's a morally relevant reason to justify treating someone differently. Based on this, vegans accept animals into the same moral sphere as humans with respect to fundamental rights, such as the right to live and the right to be free from ownership as another's property. We all belong to the animal kingdom and all animals, including humans, aren't objects. We're all sentient creatures. All animals have needs, wants, fears, abilities, intelligence, skills, social habits and emotions, which they demonstrate in ways like, and different from, humans. There are no morally relevant differences between us to justify our using animals as we currently do.

2. **What would be the answer in a human context?** – Sometimes, navigating the basic fairness principle with respect to animals can be tricky. So, whenever we find ourselves being asked about the human use of animals, or how to frame a response to an ethical question involving animals, we ask ourselves this question. The focus of the answer should be on the aggrieved or oppressed group, not the oppressor or perpetrator of the harm. In short, we

believe animals have the right to live, just as people do. Also remember, rejecting speciesism is analogous to rejecting all other forms of oppression; we understand we owe funda-mental rights of equality to those who are superficially different to us. Differences of colour, ethnicity, sex, gender, size, sexual orientation, age, ability or religion are morally irrelevant when it comes to deciding who has fundamental rights – they're inherent to all of us, including animals.

3. **Feminism** – Females of other species are exploited for their reproductive system, for no other reason than they're female. If we can't stop objectifying and oppressing female animals, how can we expect full and genuine change for women? Nonhuman animals are vulnerable and deserve inclusion in terms of feminism, fairness and the fundamen-tal right not to be exploited as an object.

4. **Race** – One of the most exploited groups of workers are those in animal agriculture, including those working in slaughterhouses. A very large number are ethnic minorities, people of colour, migrants or others in vulnerable situ-ations. If we care about race, migration and ethnicity issues, then veganism is one fitting response to those concerns.

5. **Environment** – Animal agriculture is responsible for a vast array of environmental problems, including a signifi-cant proportion of greenhouse gases. Conservatively, it's 14.5%. A fuller analysis shows animal agriculture contribut-ing 51% of greenhouse gas emissions. Fertiliser and animal faeces runoff cause dead zones in the ocean. Most of the

agricultural land is used for cultivating crops for animal feed, which is also the principal cause of deforestation and land degradation. And the plastic in the sea is mainly from discarded fishing equipment. All aspects of life on earth have been affected by animal agriculture.

6. **Health** – We don't need, at any age or stage, to eat animal products to be healthy or have delicious, nourishing and even indulgent meals. Well-respected medical and dietary institutions agree being vegan is healthy at any stage in life. It only takes a little time with any internet search engine, or a recipe book, to find how to cook even the simplest vegan meal.

7. **Cost** – If we're concerned about how to think about poverty and veganism then we need to address both, and acknowledge one doesn't preclude the other. Vegetables, grains, pulses and many fruits aren't expensive (although nuts can be). Overall, plant foods are cheaper than animal products, especially with respect to the long-term health and environmental impacts that cost more than anyone is prepared to pay.

ELEVATOR PITCH

Like us, animals aren't things. They feel, think, dream, play, have friends and families. They do these things differently than us, sure. They have different intelligence and skills than we do. And they look different from us. But so what? We all look different or live differently, and have different intelligence and skills. None of these are good enough reasons to exploit and kill anyone. All of us, human or animal, want to live. We all don't want to be exploited and used as objects. And that's why we should be vegan.

Each of these concepts and the pitch may start longer conversations, and that's a good thing. To change people's minds, we must show them a new way of thinking. To do that effectively, we must feel confident in, and comfortable with, our own thinking. We need a clear understanding of our beliefs, the courage and confidence to share them with others, and the compassion to recognise others aren't that different to us. The essays in this book not only clarify the ethical concepts underpinning veganism, they illustrate in a practical way how the concepts weave through contemporary life. Our strongest hope is for this book to become a tool fortifying your courage and increasing your confidence to go vegan in the first place and, thereafter, to talk about it with others.

CHAPTER 8

Practical Thought Experiments

The following are situations we sometimes encounter. Some are exaggerated. All are drawn from real life anecdotes. These mock encounters are meant to create a space for us to think through the issues we face as vegans or non-vegans. Some may not have clear-cut answers and some (maybe all!) will engender spirited debate. It's worthwhile spending time thinking about the answers we would give and the reasons for those answers. Questioning and examining our assumptions and logic are critical components to strengthen our resolve in being vegan, and to learn how to explain veganism to ourselves and to others. This makes us better advocates. For non-vegans, these exercises clarify where vegans are coming from.

After each scenario, there's a box with a discussion. You might choose to cover the boxes so you can think about what your own answers would be before reading ours. Apply the concepts we've discussed in this book. You might come up with the same answers or with answers in addition to, or different from, those provided. Whatever you conclude, think about why.

We'd love to hear your scenarios, questions and conundrums! Email us at ThinkLikeAVeganBook@gmail.com or contact us through our social media: ThinkLikeAVegan.

1. Joshua is outraged by stories in the news about abused or abandoned cats, dogs and horses, animals going extinct, orcas dying in aquariums, zoo animals getting shot, foxes being hunted, dog fighting or racing, horse racing and all other types of animal cruelty.

Joshua goes home and drowns their sorrows with a double bacon cheeseburger, a glass of milk and a slice of cheesecake.

a. Is there a morally relevant difference between the animals whose lives Joshua feels sympathy for and wants to see preserved or safeguarded and those animals Joshua uses for food?

> There's no morally relevant difference between dogs, cats, horses, foxes, orcas, pandas, orangutans, chickens, cows, sheep, rabbits, goats and any other non-human animal. They're all sentient. We may be more familiar with some and not others, or in awe of some over others. Admittedly, some have been bred, historically, while some are companions or pets; others are wild, and some may be rare or endangered (due to human action and activity); they may be variously considered cute, dumb, smart, fuzzy or ugly. Whatever the case may be, all those qualities are judgements, decisions, thoughts and actions we make or take. They have nothing to do with the animals themselves. The animals all want to live and none of them are objects for us to own.

b. Joshua doesn't kill animals for food. They buy animal products at the shop. Alternatively, Joshua only eats animal products from animals they kill. Does either of these variations make any difference?

No, there's no difference. Whether we directly kill animals, or ask someone else to do it for us, doesn't change the outcome for the animal. The moral problem remains because the animal is exploited and losing their life. Even if we don't kill them directly, our demand for their bodily products means someone else will slaughter them on our behalf to meet that demand.

2. Shiro doesn't like, and fears, animals. Shiro is also scared of people they don't know. Nevertheless, Shiro wants everyone to be treated fairly and injustice doesn't sit well with them.
a. Do you have to like people to be fair to them?

No. Our personal preferences are just that: personal. They have no bearing on issues of fundamental fairness. Just because you may dislike us personally doesn't mean you wish for us to be treated unfairly. Perhaps you do have that wish, but that's a whole different kettle of chips beyond the scope of this book!

b. Do you have to like animals to be fair to them?

The same principle applies with respect to animals. We don't need to particularly like animals to want them to be treated fairly. Whether we like them, are terrified of them, allergic or even uninterested in them has no bearing on whether we should be fair to them. Being fair to animals means they have the right to live without being exploited as objects. Our likes, dislikes, fears, allergies or disinterest have all to do with us and our perceptions, not with the animals themselves.

c. Do you have to like animals to be vegan?

We can be vegan and not like animals. As we've just discussed, there's no prerequisite to like any animal to be fair to them.

3. Tembi detests hunting. They support proposed legislation to stop hunting and they go to protests. Tembi also supports sabotaging hunts. Tembi isn't vegan though and likes bacon, steak and eggs. Tembi believes they're addicted to cheese. Tembi is cutting back on meat consumption so they skip eating meat on Mondays.

a. What are some of the issues here and why?

Whether there's a morally relevant reason for Tembi to be against hunting whilst continuing to eat and use animal products.

No, there's no morally relevant reason to differentiate between animals who are hunted and those farmed for food. Although Tembi wants to reduce the suffering of some animals through their activism, which is a good thing, Tembi's diet is contributing to the needless suffering and death of many other animals. Tembi's diet is also continuing to contribute to environmental degradation and the exploitation of humans.

Whether Tembi's choices of activism square with their being non-vegan.

People hunt for the various pleasures connected to that activity. Tembi indirectly employs others to kill animals for their pleasure of eating. The common denominator between Tembi and the hunter is their pleasure with respect to each of their chosen activities. Our pleasure is a completely subjective and self-serving motivation for an action and not a morally relevant reason for animals to die or be exploited as objects. Tembi's activism comes from a place of wanting to do good or choose the right action. It doesn't make moral sense for Tembi to be both against hunting and pro eating animal products. Choosing which animal we hunt for sport and which we use for food is an arbitrary choice. Neither is necessary. Tembi might better advance the cause of stopping hunting if they became vegan, and discussed the reasons for veganism with others.

Whether Tembi's once a week abstention from meat is sufficient.

Although there's some good in that, it's difficult to quantify the relevance or impact of such a short-term action. Tembi might still consume dairy or eggs on that day, or to compensate, they might increase their animal foods consumption later in the week.

Whether cheese addiction is a morally relevant reason to continue eating dairy cheese.

With respect to cheese addiction, we're sceptical there would be physical withdrawal symptoms as one would experience when stopping powerful narcotics, alcohol or nicotine. Besides, even if there were, addiction wouldn't be a morally relevant reason to deny another's fundamental rights.

4. Alex is vegan and happens to be visiting a part of town without a vegan restaurant, shop or café. There are other cafés, a corner shop and a small supermarket.

a. What are some things Alex might do?

It's frustrating for any vegan to be somewhere where suitable food is unavailable. Alex could stop in the local corner shop or supermarket to buy an apple, banana, some crisps, nuts or even bread – anything vegan to tide them over until they reach home or elsewhere with more options. Local shops are often the easiest and cheapest options in such cases.

While they're in the shop, Alex might also want to consider looking around to see if there are canned or frozen vegetables, beans and fruits, as well as looking for what different types of grains might be available to those who live in the area. Understanding food apartheid will be helpful in identifying the socio-political and economic dimension of food politics in the area. If indeed plant-based foods in whatever form are unavailable, then Alex might think about what it may be like for people who live in that area with respect to the food choices available to them, and how that affects the lives of those people.

It's unfortunate this area has no vegan restaurants. But this doesn't mean Alex is out of luck. Alex could pop into a reasonable-looking eatery and ask if they might prepare something plant-based for them, even if it's just a lettuce salad or jacket potato (that's a baked potato for our North American friends). Many eateries anywhere in the world are amenable to preparing something plant-based if requested.

Alex might also want to carry some snacks for just such emergencies.

b. How does this inconvenience affect Alex's decisions?

Alex's temporary situation and discomfort may affect the pleasure they derive from eating on that day, or in that moment. Their temporary discomfort doesn't change whether Alex has a moral obligation towards animals.

c. Do we always need elaborate foods?

Alex can choose to eat something simple on this day. We don't need for every meal to be a complicated affair. It's okay for food to be boring every now and again, or even all the time if that's the only choice we have. In many places, staple diets of grains, beans and vegetables, with the occasional fruit, are standard for most people.

d. Might Alex go for a non-vegan meal?

Unless there's a real life-or-death situation for Alex, there is no need for them to actively choose to eat a non-vegan meal. It's not likely Alex would perish if they were to miss just one meal in this particular circumstance.

e. Should Alex just give up being vegan?

Of course not, just as Alex wouldn't give up being against sexism or ageism because they have a particularly bad day.

f. Does this mean it's hard to be vegan? If so, who bears the hardship?

Alex's predicament is certainly frustrating, but they have other options. They'll almost certainly be able to eat foods other than those containing animal products. If it's difficult to be vegan in some circumstances, for example when we experience inconveniences such as Alex's, or we face social and family pressures or unpleasant interactions, then we must compare these difficulties of ours to the immense suffering and death billions of animals experience each year.

g. Is there anything special or heroic at play here in Alex's behaviour?

Alex isn't a hero for staying vegan, just like Alex wouldn't be a hero for staying non-sexist. Veganism is an outward manifestation of not being speciesist. It's the most effective and yet basic thing we can do for the animals. We owe being vegan to the animals, just as we owe people not to be racist, sexist, ableist, classist, ageist or homophobic. Of course, even without a hero's cape, Alex may justifiably feel good or have a sense of accomplishment about navigating a new situation, especially if they're recently vegan.

h. Does it make any difference if Alex is in a foreign country?

No. There are many resources facilitating being vegan in another country, including books and apps, each with the basic concept of veganism translated into many languages. A bit of basic research before travelling goes a long way.

5. Comet is on public transport, sitting next to a woman wearing a fur coat. Comet is also sitting next to a man wearing a wool suit and overcoat, silk tie, leather shoes and carrying a leather briefcase.

Across from Comet is a man wearing a parka with a hood trimmed with fur and he's with a woman wearing a parka filled with feathers or down, and next to them there's another man wearing a leather biker jacket.

Comet only gives the side-eye to and insults the woman wearing fur, and doesn't seem to notice the others.

a. Why might Comet be reacting this way?

Comet's reaction to fur is understandable to an extent because fur hits us on a visual and visceral basis. Their overall reaction is puzzling though. Perhaps it's because over the years we've been conditioned to only think about, or be offended by, fur because the campaigns against it are so visible and have garnered so much publicity. Also, it's easy to pick on fur because it's not something most people use, despite the proliferation of fur-trimmed parkas.

b. Is there any morally relevant difference between fur, leather, wool, feathers or silk?

None is morally worse than the other. All these products are the result of animals being used as objects or resources and being killed. The way exploitation and death are conducted or administered is immaterial to the fundamental question of whether animals should be used in the first place. Condemning only fur where people are wearing leather, wool, feathers and silk reinforces the idea using animals for fur is somehow morally worse than using them for any other product. It also gives a pass to people wearing other animals because they won't feel the need to think about their moral choices. People can feel smug about fur, maintaining they'd *never do such a thing*. Very few would ever give a passing thought to any of their other clothing, such as a woollen jumper.

c. Might there be a sexist aspect to this situation, however subconscious?

It's worth considering this question because it's women who most often wear fur. Attacking or criticising women for choices they make, while ignoring or being quiet about men who make morally equivalent choices, is at the heart of sexism and even misogyny. Accepting such disparate treatment between men and women under the guise of being pro-animal is unfortunate and unfair.

6. Xenos is at a colleague's house. Xenos forgot to inform the host they're vegan. The host has some suitable food they could prepare. But, Xenos opts to eat the non-vegan food because they don't want to offend the host. Later, when a few people at the table start telling bigoted jokes, Xenos doesn't laugh or participate.

a. What might be some of the issues here and why?

There are two important issues to think about: whether Xenos has any morally relevant reason to compromise being vegan at this dinner and whether Xenos not participating in bigotry also offends the host.

Going to someone's house who may be unaware their guest is vegan puts the host in a predicament. Xenos is also in a tough spot because they forgot to mention it to their host. So, yes, this is a socially awkward situation and it's likely to result in both people feeling uncomfortable. Eating the non-vegan meal might spare the host some initial discomfort. But saving face, whether theirs or the host's, isn't a good reason for Xenos to compromise down by discounting or disregarding animals' lives or any related issues. Xenos' compromise places a higher value on the host's feelings instead of lives. Xenos has compromised fairness for no good reason.

When it comes to human-related bigotry, Xenos makes a conscious choice not to engage in that because Xenos understands it's the right thing to do. Whether the host takes offence is irrelevant to Xenos. Although silence may sometimes indicate complicity or appeasement, silence might be the only thing Xenos feels they can do in the circumstances. Alternatively, Xenos might take this opportunity to speak up, or cross his arms in silence and disapproval, or respond in another way. This will be Xenos' choice based on their own experiences and the situation they face.

b. Why might Xenos have reacted differently in these situations?

Xenos might still harbour latent speciesism, despite being vegan, and offending a person might seem worse to them than using or consuming animal products. Speciesism is the norm, after all. Speciesism is what makes it possible for people to differentiate which animal they'll keep and love as part of their family, and which they'll exploit or kill. It's clear we live in a world with systemic oppression of people based on class, race, gender, sexual orientation, age, physical ability and appearance. We must also acknowledge the systemic oppression of non-humans based on species. Systemic oppression builds prejudices and -isms all around us. We absorb them passively without even realising it. An important step in dismantling oppression is to identify and unlearn such misguided notions residing within ourselves. This process is necessary to effect transformative change, although it can be difficult and sometimes painful. It would be valuable to Xenos to contemplate their reasons for the different reactions.

c. What, if anything, might Xenos have done differently?

Xenos could have apologised for the oversight and offered to prepare or help prepare something with what the host had on hand.

If Xenos had remembered to inform the host about being vegan, they could have offered to prepare and bring a dish to contribute to the meal and share with others, or offered the host some example recipes. Potentially, these exchanges and the different food might have sparked a conversation about veganism with the host or other guests.

7. At a vegan festival Sandi brings their rescue alpaca, George. Sandi and George walk around the festival grounds. Everyone loves George. He's super cute and everyone wants their photo with him. The next year, festival organisers hire a pig, chicken, alpaca and cow from a sanctuary so people can take their picture with the animals.

a.   What might be some of the issues here and why?

There are two principal issues here: whether it's okay to use animals for human entertainment and whether intent changes the answer. First, although it's great for Sandi to rescue an alpaca, is it in George's best interest to be in a crowded and noisy place? We hope Sandi would put the alpaca's best interests first before any personal gain.

Second, using animals for entertainment isn't good. Animals shouldn't be taken out of a safe, natural or familiar environment and put on display to please people. This includes animals trained to behave in a certain way to entertain us. Animals can't effectively give their consent to being used like this. They're not adult humans (or even old-enough children) with all their mental faculties, who can decide for themselves whether they want to participate. We wouldn't, or at least agree we shouldn't, display or use as entertainment a person who hasn't consented, or who can't. Animals don't understand entertainment like people do. When we use animals for entertainment, we're exploiting them, even if we're treating them well and they appear to live good lives. As we've discussed, good treatment doesn't solve the problem of our using them in the first place.

It's easy to identify zoos, circuses, aquariums, or horse and dog racing tracks as places whose primary existence depends on animal exploitation. These places and activities are entrenched in our world just as much as eating animals is.

A word about training dogs or other companion animals. Training dogs to behave in a certain way arises from a necessity for the dog to fit into our world. Dogs are perfectly happy doing dog things. Because we've domesticated them to live in such proximity to us, their behaviour, for better or worse, must conform to our lives. If a dog doesn't behave as we'd like them to, then that dog loses. They'll become a *problem* dog and it might lead to them being abandoned or killed.

Our reasoning doesn't mean we shouldn't adopt animals or train them. Of course, we should adopt dogs or cats, fish, rabbits, alpacas or whoever, and train them for their own safety. We must also be conscious and mindful of the problems inherent in that relationship. There's no easy answer to this other than for us to stop breeding animals for our own purposes and enjoyment.

As for art, film or theatre, the same problems arise. Why do we need to use animals in these pursuits? We wouldn't use a person if they couldn't consent. Do we have a good reason to reconcile our pursuits with their inability to effectively consent? Do our own preferences make it acceptable to use animals to fulfil our artistic or story-telling desires? What does it do for and to them? There may not be perfect answers here, but these are questions we should be asking.

b. Does it make any difference if the festival charges for the time spent with the animals?

We don't think so. Only our squeamishness or discomfort with money might make it seem less appealing to us. The animals don't care about money. The festival is exploiting the animals to draw people in and to provide entertainment.

c. Does it make a difference if the only request is to donate to the sanctuary?

Once again, we don't think so. Appeasing our discomfort with a charitable donation is all about us feeling better about using the animals.

d. Does it make a difference if the festival had not hired a sanctuary? Or hired a farmer to bring their animals? What if these types of events are the only way the sanctuary can raise funds to keep the animals in liveable conditions?

Set aside any opinions about farmers, sanctuaries or money, and instead ask yourself a simple question: is there a morally relevant reason to use animals? In this case, it makes no difference whether the festival hired a professional animal keeper instead of a sanctuary, or even hired a farmer. Perhaps the sanctuary's or the keeper's animals are better treated than on the farm, but this doesn't make it right to use the animals in the first place. Of course, if the festival had decided it was going to use the animals anyway, then they might prefer the sanctuary animals over the others.

Some might say the presence of animals is educational. Does education have to come at the expense of animals? There are other ways to educate. We study so many things without experiencing them, yet we make exceptions for animals. Must we physically see and bear witness to animals to realise they are worthy of life? Perhaps there are valid arguments in some circumstances and we might want to think about what those might be. We owe it to the animals to start asking ourselves these questions.

There are so many animals – because we breed them into existence – who need sanctuary. Sanctuaries are expensive operations, so the need for money is understandable. If these events are the only income for the sanctuary, we're once again faced with similar uncomfortable questions and few hard answers. Such discomfort and imperfect answers point to one simple, concrete action: choosing veganism.

8. Karl is ill. They have cancer, or a treatable virus or a

bacterial infection, or they're diabetic, or simply have a headache or allergies. They need to take medications to function. The medications may or may not be vegan.

a. What might be some of the issues here and why?

There are two main issues here: whether being vegan means one can't take medication and whether Karl's need for medications makes them non-vegan, or a lesser or failing vegan.

Karl's medication is the only way by which they can survive or function as best they can. We live in a world where animal products are, sadly, used in a variety of applications, including medicine. It's debatable whether medicine requires animal products for manufacturing or to be effective, but we accept, for this argument, it does. Karl may not have access to a vegan substitute of a medicine or one might not exist at all.

As we discussed in Chapter 1, being vegan means avoiding using animals *to the extent possible and practicable*. In this case, Karl can't avoid consuming something containing an animal product, or it's not practicable for them to do so because there's no viable alternative to their medication.

In a different world where animals weren't considered objects or commodities, their use in medicine wouldn't exist or, if absolutely necessary, it would be limited. Until this happens, we must navigate a life fraught with serious and sometimes unresolvable ethical conflicts. Karl continues to be vegan. They're not less vegan because they need medication containing animal products, and the existence of these conflicts doesn't mean we can't or shouldn't be vegan in our daily lives despite these challenges.

9. Fina has just discovered their local currency notes contain traces of animal products. Fina owns a vegan shop. They decide their business will refuse the notes and only accept electronic payments.

    After this decision, Fina walks over to their local market. The market isn't vegan and neither are any of the suppliers or their farmers. Fina pays with their debit card.

    Then, Fina goes home or to their office. Fina doesn't know what type of insulation or what sorts of building materials were used because Fina didn't build the structures. It's likely one or both contain animal products, such as wool.

    Fina walks on the streets, which are paved with tarmac. And Fina sometimes drives an old, used or rental car and these have leather seats. More often, Fina takes a bus. Fina has heard there are animal products used in tarmac, tyres and other parts of automotive vehicles.

    a. What might be some of the issues facing Fina and why? How does *to the extent possible and practicable* apply here?

    The principal issue here is similar to Karl's in the previous scenario: whether being vegan means we can no longer use those ubiquitous items containing animal products when there aren't viable alternatives.

Although it's a perfectly acceptable personal choice to use or not use something necessary and ubiquitous containing animal products (such as money or roads), we're no less vegan for continuing to do so. Abstaining from using the item doesn't make anyone a special vegan hero or more committed to veganism than any other vegan. The enormous global demand for animal products results in so much *excess* animal by-products. Because they're so plentiful, they're also inexpensive and are purchased as components or ingredients in a variety of manufacturing applications.

This doesn't mean we can't be vegan in a non-vegan world. It simply means we often have no choice but to indirectly engage with animal products, the pervasiveness of which should be remarkable to anyone. Any time we spend money, we may be indirectly supporting animal use or other forms of exploitation or suffering we wouldn't otherwise support, and the same is true for anyone, vegan or non, who spends money anywhere.

In the world in which we live, we have limited ways of reconciling any of these problems with our ethics. Once again, we must remember the *to the extent possible and practicable* part of the definition of veganism. We can't live without money. We can't avoid shopping in a market or buying vegan products from non-vegans, or riding on buses or in cars containing animal products, or even the simple act of walking on a tarmacked street. These are the simple realities of the deeply imperfect and unjust world in which we live. One way to tackle these imperfections and dismantle the injustices is to recognise them, learn about them, reject them from our lives wherever possible, make others aware of them and build on that to demand systemic change.

10. Solly rants against the Chinese over an annual dog meat festival and against the Japanese for whale and dolphin hunting. Solly isn't vegan.

Sometime later, Solly goes vegan and wants to become an activist. Solly still rants against the Chinese and Japanese. Solly says nothing about the millions of animals slaughtered in Solly's own country (where Solly wouldn't get arrested for speaking their mind).

Solly has a friend, Moon, who isn't vegan. Moon tells Solly they're vegan twice a week. Solly says to Moon, 'Good! At least you're doing something.'

a. What might be some of the issues before and after Solly goes vegan?

There are two important issues here. First, whether there are any morally relevant differences for Solly to distinguish between the animals they consume and dogs, whales or dolphins. Second, and this persists after Solly goes vegan, whether Solly has any morally relevant reason to distinguish between any nationality or culture when it comes to consuming animal products when doing so is something all nationalities, cultures and ethnicities do.

b. Might there be an element of xenophobia or racism (conscious or unconscious) at work here?

Sadly, we believe there might be. What matters is with respect to consuming animal products; there's no morally relevant difference between people who eat them, regardless of location, nationality, ethnicity, religion, culture or another qualifier. People in China or Japan are no different than people in the US or Europe. A dog steak is no different than a cow steak, no matter how strange either one may appear to us. The problem Solly identifies isn't related to ethnicity, nationality or which animal someone is hunting or eating. The real problem is animal use, which is a global norm.

c. Is there a morally relevant difference between dogs, chicken, whales and dolphins slaughtered on specific occasions and cows, chickens or fish slaughtered daily?

We believe there's no difference between them, whether they're slaughtered on a specific occasion or daily for conventional foods. It's all equally sad, unnecessary and unfair. Focusing on charismatic animals or specific occasions only highlights tangential issues of *who* and *when*. Often, this focus devolves into demonising particular cultures, ethnicities, religions or nationalities. This doesn't mean Solly must accept these events. On the contrary, Solly is justified in being upset about all animal use whenever it occurs. They can use these occurrences as opportunities to demonstrate we shouldn't be using animals in the first place.

d. Might there be a problem with what Solly said to Moon? Might Solly have said something different to Moon?

It's very good to be supportive of Moon's decision. But must the conversation end there? Would the conversation end like that if it were, for example, about not being bigoted twice a week? Probably not. In this case, in addition to a supportive response, Solly might consider sharing with Moon additional positive aspects of eating vegan food, trying new products, or some personal anecdote about Solly's own experience of becoming vegan and maybe even their own vegan elevator pitch! Of course, all conversations depend on context. Let's just remember there's always space to compromise up.

e. What types of activism might Solly choose to undertake?

At the 2020 Women of the World Festival, we heard a talk with Angela Davis, American political activist, philosopher, scholar, author and vegan.[1]

She had three suggestions for engaging in activism: own our talents, develop ourselves (not everyone wants to be an organiser), and question how we can express our own individuality in the process of pushing forward a collective endeavour. Solly's activism doesn't need to be exclusively protest or street activism. The more Solly informs themselves and talks to people, educating them about being vegan, the more it's likely Solly will find people who are interested in thinking about the issues, or who show an interest in changing their diet. Solly may only be comfortable speaking with people whom they know personally, or they might enjoy the challenge of organising events. Solly may meet like-minded people with whom they could collaborate and organise. If Solly has talents, like art, music, writing or whatever else, they might be able to incorporate those talents into their activism. And if Solly isn't interested in any conventional activism, then this is okay too. Living life as a vegan is sometimes all the activism one can, or may want to, handle.

11. Zammy buys a dog from a breeder. Zammy might not be vegan. Their vegan friends are disappointed Zammy didn't adopt, but they play with the dog. Zammy says to their friends, 'You hate my dog!'

a. What might we consider with respect to dog breeding?

Although in many parts of the world people have a different relationship with dogs, cats or other companion animals than they might have with cows or other farm animals, we must separate these personal feelings from the way we think about the matter. It's important we look at whether there's any morally relevant reason to distinguish between, for example, breeding a dog and breeding a cow. We breed cows for profit and to exploit their bodies, whether for labour, dairy milk, meat or leather. These reasons suit us as people and have nothing to do with the cows themselves. We breed dogs, or other companion animals, primarily for profit and companionship, sometimes for labour such as farming and hunting, and occasionally for sport. Again, these reasons suit us as people and have nothing to do with the dogs themselves. In both instances, we view the animal as an object to own and exploit for what the animal can give us, be it the pleasure we derive from their company, or the food we eat from a farm animal. We must once again remind ourselves these benefits are about *us* and *not* the animals themselves. If there's no morally relevant difference between people and animals in terms of the fundamental right not to be treated as an object, then we have no good reason to forcibly or artificially breed any animal, whether for profit, food or companionship. Instead and if we can, we should adopt or foster one or more of the vast numbers of animals who need our help and protection.

b. Do Zammy's friends hate the dog because Zammy didn't adopt them?

Although they would've preferred Zammy adopt a dog instead of buying one, they don't hate the dog. The dog has nothing to do with Zammy's decision to buy them, or with the fact people breed animals for their own purposes. The dog only wants one thing: to live.

c. If Zammy were vegan, why might they purchase a dog from a breeder? Might there be a good reason to do so?

Perhaps Zammy hasn't thought about the implications of purchasing a dog, or not considered the connection between buying and breeding a sentient being and the millions of animals who are abandoned. Zammy may have only focused on themselves and what they wanted, which is the problem in a nutshell.

Although we wouldn't purchase any animal, some people will purchase animals to then *save* or *rescue* them, such as chickens or pigs from farms, slaughterhouses or live animal markets. There's an argument for doing this, of course, but despite the motivation to do so coming from a very good place, it's not without consequences. For example, buying rescue animals sometimes encourages a new market to form around such rescues, with animals being bred for *rescue* sales. There's no easy or comfortable answer to this, other than to follow your heart and to be mindful of the impact of your actions.

d. What might Zammy's vegan friends do to help them be vegan and adopt instead of buy?

Zammy's vegan friends might talk with them about veganism. They might help them cook vegan meals and demonstrate to them the parallels between all animals. They might show

Zammy how many animals need loving homes or introduce them to good rescue or fostering organisations. The opportunities and permutations of what Zammy's friends might do to help educate them are endless. Will Zammy become vegan or adopt an animal? Who knows! But Zammy's friends can try. It will then be up to Zammy to make these choices.

12. Kush is Janna's parent. Janna is six years old. They're both vegan. Kush tells Janna when they get older, they should try meat to see what it's like. They also tell Janna they don't care what Janna does outside the house as long as they're vegan in the house.

a. Why might Kush say this?

Perhaps Kush hasn't thought through the impact of their words on Janna or about the ethical questions concerning veganism. There's no need for anyone to taste animal products to become vegan. Tasting an animal product isn't going to persuade someone one way or another about the ethical reasons for *not* using animals. We may like the taste of animal products or we may not. Taste makes no difference as to whether we have a right to use them.

We don't believe there's a good reason for Kush not to encourage Janna to be vegan inside and outside of their house. Janna might be feeling outside pressure at school or with friends about being vegan, and of course, Janna will do whatever a child wants to do when a parent isn't around; we've all been there! Equipping Janna or any child with the best possible knowledge, encouragement and support is something all parents would hope to give to their children, if possible. Similarly, in a human context, Kush wouldn't encourage Janna to be bigoted outside the home, and this is also applicable to veganism. If children understand the reasons for their actions and beliefs, and they know they're supported and cared for by the adults in their lives, they'll hopefully make the best ethical choices, including being vegan both inside and outside the home. And they'll need this sense of security when they navigate adolescence and teenage years.

b. Can children understand the basic ethics behind veganism?

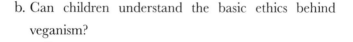

Most six-year-old children (and probably younger) are likely to be able to understand what's fair and unfair, at least at a basic level. Because the essential principles of veganism are based in fairness, children have the capacity to grasp why they'd want to be fair to animals. Consequently, they'll understand how being vegan would be part of being fair, especially if the concepts are explained to them in straightforward terms.

13. Gombe is vegan and they receive a non-vegan lip balm as a gift. Although Gombe wouldn't buy or use this product,

they'd like someone who isn't vegan to make use of it. Gombe regifts the lip balm because they don't like waste and would rather have someone use than discard it. Gombe feels good about this because they didn't support the initial exploitation of an animal. Because the product already exists, Gombe feels there's no harm involved in giving it away.

a. Is regifting a non-vegan item different from purchasing a non-vegan item?

Although it seems like a *waste*, Gombe might want to consider binning the lip balm. In both cases, we're using the products of an animal. The only difference here is there isn't any money exchanged in regifting. That animal was exploited either directly for that item, in terms of eggs and dairy in a non-vegan cake, for example, or indirectly as a component of an object, in terms of the lip balm in this case. Does it matter it's only a lip balm, and not tyres for a car or a computer or a mobile phone? Yes, it matters. A non-vegan lip balm is an easily substituted item, whereas tyres, computers or mobile phones, all of which may contain non-vegan components, may be impossible or impracticable to substitute. In addition, the latter are necessary to the world we live in today, which brings us right back to the *possible and practicable* part of the definition of the term vegan we discussed previously.

b. What might we want to think about when regifting or promoting a non-essential, non-vegan product to our non-vegan friends and family? Are non-vegans able to make the distinctions vegans hope they would make?

On the one hand, we want people to understand not using animals is a moral baseline for everyone, and our living without animal products is very important to us. On the other, we might be confusing people by gifting or promoting non-essential, non-vegan items. How are our non-vegan friends and families meant to react next time we say we don't want the non-vegan cookie? Or when we kindly refuse to accept another non-vegan item from them? Consistency in our beliefs and ethics is important. If we're inconsistent, this might result in a friend or family member responding something like, 'Well, you gave me non-vegan lip balm, so I thought it was all the same to you.'

We may have decided to regift the item because of our efforts to reduce waste, but even if our non-vegan friends and family understood we were making an exception in this case, they may not remember that next time. In the long run, they might only remember we gave them a non-vegan item. On some level, it *is* wasteful to dispose of a non-vegan product instead of using it. But does this matter? After all, it's also unjust and unfair to *waste* the life of a sentient being to make a lip balm, cake or other non-vegan item when it's perfectly possible to make these things with vegan ingredients. It's a *waste* so many products are manufactured with the complete disregard for animal lives and for any human who may also suffer or be exploited in the process. Our demand for animal products has so many different negative impacts. If we tackle demand by keeping our vegan message clear, perhaps we'll have a more meaningful and lasting impact than a momentary waste of a lip balm.

c. What about buying thrifted animal products (a vintage leather jacket or woollen jumper)?

A similar thought process applies here as with regifting or promoting non-vegan items. Is the item a necessity? Are there suitable vegan alternatives in the charity shop? If there aren't alternatives and it's a necessity, then it's an instance of the imperfect choices we sometimes have to make. What about the items we already have? Not everyone has the means to replace all their non-vegan clothing with suitable clothing or it might be impracticable or impossible for a variety of reasons (and the same applies to household items, such as leather sofas). Someone might be unable to immediately replace a necessary item of clothing, like a woollen winter coat for example, or they might never be able to do so. This doesn't mean the person is less vegan. It does mean sending mixed messages though. But even that can be a positive springboard for conversation about the fundamentals of veganism.

14. Sibo is vegan. They eat a new vegan burger. Before being able to sell the burger, the manufacturer was obliged to test some of the ingredients on animals because of government regulations. This happened years prior to Sibo eating it. The company is no longer testing on animals. Sibo also eats vegetables and fruits picked by workers who

are likely to have been subject to exploitation and those fruits and vegetables are brought to market on the back of donkeys. Sibo might not realise any of these things.

a. Is there a moral difference between the use of animals for testing or the use of animals in fruit and vegetable agriculture?

No. In both cases, animals are used as objects and the problem is with their use. Of course, there may be differences in the relative pain or suffering animals used in testing may endure in comparison to *beasts of burden*, but maybe not. Neither is a particularly good life and all involve exploitation and eventual slaughter. It's an awful life for all these animals. The moral question is separate from whether either the company or the farmer could've made different choices in manufacturing or bringing their product to market, whether a traditional market with stalls or our supermarket shelves. They made their decisions based on what they believed they must do to make a living. Remember, we live in a non-vegan world where using animals as tools to make or bring products to market is the norm.

b. Does any of this make Sibo any less vegan?

No. The burger is a plant-based food. The vegetables and fruit are, obviously, plant-based foods. The food and the animal use to bring the food to market are two separate moral issues and shouldn't be conflated.

c. Does it matter morally whether Sibo knows about the animal use or testing? If so, how?

It's a moral matter only as a separate consideration from whether the food is suitable for vegans. If they know, Sibo may feel they no longer want the burger or the fruit or vegetable. But they may also feel it's not practicable or possible to not have or eat those products. The answer will depend on Sibo's situation; the availability of and access to alternatives, as well as other factors.

d. Does the exploitation of people make the vegetables and fruits any less suitable for vegans?

Similarly to the discussion above, no. Those plant products are still suitable for vegans. The human issue exists and must be addressed. But once again, Sibo might not have access to other foods. This neither makes the human issue any less important nor the food any less vegan. Knowing such human exploitation exists is a critical component of our opposition to it and for the fight to eradicate it.

15. Fengmian is vegan and is invited to a charity cooking event. The event benefits a group of refugees from a war-torn nation. The food everyone will be cooking together at the event is non-vegan. The organisers have included a note saying vegan food can be made available upon request. Fengmian has no other way of supporting this cause about which they care a great deal.

a. Why might this event make Fengmian feel uneasy, and how might they respond?

Fengmian makes an analogy to a human context. Fengmian imagines a benefit event against sexism, where homophobic imagery and art is used as the central event theme. If guests don't want to see that imagery or art, they can opt out by sitting at a different table. It makes no sense to Fengmian to fight the injustice perpetrated against refugees, who are fleeing the terrors of war, by cooking products from animals who experience a similar state of terror and are themselves subject to injustice and death.

As always, there are a variety of responses. For example, Fengmian might share their human context analogy with their friend or the organisation. Or they might inform them that, although they support the cause and are happy there are vegan options, they're disappointed the core group mission of fairness and justice doesn't extend to all sentient beings.

b. Might the answer be different if cooking wasn't central to the event? For instance, if it were a benefit music event where dinner also happened to be served?

There are a variety of options open to Fengmian. They understand speciesism is everywhere. It's systemic. If the event weren't focused on cooking or if the food were just one part of the evening, then they might feel less uneasy because the centre of attention would be something other than the non-vegan ingredients.

However, Fengmian might decide they'll choose the vegan option and attend the cooking event because they support the cause. They believe having at least one vegan at the event would be better than having no vegans. In addition, Fengmian hopes they might have a chance to have conversations with other guests and influence someone's perspective about veganism.

Alternatively, Fengmian might decide they'll not attend the event, but they'll contribute to the cause.

16. Pallas is discussing veganism with Bia. Pallas is on fire and answering all Bia's questions, providing point and counterpoint, debunking myths and all the while being compassionate and understanding. At the end of the conversation, Bia tells Pallas they don't care and have no intention of going vegan. Pallas is disappointed. What can they do?

Unfortunately, nothing. Disappointment and even sadness are natural responses. Pallas managed to have an exchange and that's good. Perhaps the discussion planted seeds or addressed concerns or fears Bia had which they'll think about more on their own. Or perhaps Bia will relay the conversation to someone else and that person might become interested. There are myriad possibilities. An angry response will be counterproductive, as will animosity. We can't change others; that's not within our control. We can discuss, explain, show a different perspective and share our experiences. Pallas can look for people who will be receptive or interested in learning more about veganism. Change is an individual matter, and unless we've been vegan all our lives, each one of us was or has been in Bia's place to some extent.

Further Reading

To delve deeper into the basic ideas related to veganism we've explored in this book, we recommend the works of Tom Regan, Gary Francione and Anna Charlton, Sherry Colb and Michael Dorf, David Nibert and Carol J. Adams. Their works aren't the only influences on our thinking about fairness and social issues. That list is long, so here are a few modern writers and thinkers for your consideration: Maya Angelou, Angela Davis, Hannah Arendt, James Baldwin, Kimberlé Crenshaw, Stewart Hall, bell hooks, Carlo Levi, Primo Levi, Audre Lorde, Toni Morrison, Ida B. Wells, Mary Wollstone-craft, and Malcolm X.

Authors' Notes

From Emilia

Thank you to all those who have been with us during many steps in the making of this book and have been our ears for so many discussions.

Thank you to Roger Leese, whose love and support sustains me, for being the sunshine of my life, always challenging my thinking and enduring with humour and grace two years of playing second fiddle to this project; Eva Charalambides for inspiring and agreeing to undertake this adventure with boundless humour, creativity and unwavering conviction that together we could make this happen, and for being a true sister-friend; Cheryl Ashman for being there always and through everything; Lucy Austen for asking questions which became an impetus for this project; Rob Broder for being a sounding board for all my leaps of faith since our 1980s radio days; Foppe de Haan for his validating thumbs-up to a very early draft; Kip Dorrell, who listens to me prattle on endlessly with humour and great patience, for her incisive and thoughtful comments steering me to think and express myself more clearly; Lisa Forbes for pushing me (giving me no choice actually) to create workshops, take them on the road and being the camera person during a workshop held on the hottest day in Berlin; Paigan Hall for coming up with the original working title and graphics and being one of the funniest people I've ever met; Carol Leister for being an unwavering cheerleader, earliest draft reader and sharing helpful tips from her own publishing experience; Kay Kay Li for being inquisitive and adding dimension to many scenarios; Damon McDonald for all our conversations about veganism making me a better advocate and for being a tireless advocate himself; Emma Osborne for her infectious enthusiasm, resolve and creativity, propelling me into unknown territory and for connecting us with Unbound; Jane Patterson and Sebastiano Cossia Castiglioni for their incredible hospitality, superlative generosity, unflagging encouragement and friendship; Seth Tibbott, whose friendship is a treasured gift, for his invaluable experience, insight and suggestions on a number of drafts and for his unflagging belief in, and enthusiasm for, this project which made my soul soar; Ashley Wilson for being an assiduous vegan pizza and panettone tester and providing fresh perspectives on my work; Peggy Warren for so many discussions about life and veganism, her positivity and for inspiring me to find opportunities for advocacy anywhere and everywhere; and Marika Weinhardt for her excellent environmental advice.

From Eva

My first thank you goes to you, the reader, for taking the time to *Think Like a Vegan*. Whether you are curious about veganism or are simply a supporter of Emilia and myself (or both), I hope that you'll feel empowered to take action by the time you reach the back cover.

Thank you to my husband, Matt, for whom all my ideas are strained through and sweetened; a man so giving that even the immortality of this acknowledgement page feels small. Everything I am is due in part to your love, support and unwavering ambition to beat me at vegan cooking and baking. Thank you, Emilia, for being the kind of best friend who gets mistaken for family by strangers, someone twice as beautiful as the clearest moonbow and who has enriched my life with more sustenance than even the deepest bowl of her legendary clapshot could. With so many beautiful memories between us, I look forward to seeing how we'll possibly one-up publishing a book together in the future. Thank you to my companion animals, Libby and Dorito, for helping me advocate for veganism and for guaranteeing there's never an overripe banana in the house. Thank you to every individual that has, whether consciously or unconsciously, encouraged this learning tool into existence. I hold a deep gratitude for those who fight alongside us for the equality of all living beings and I can only hope that our ideas become the norm as others come to understand the true power of their own actions.

From both of us

This book would not exist without the generosity of all those who believed in us and supported us in the Unbound campaign. The outpouring of encouragement, kind words and material support moved us daily. We had no idea crowdfunding for this book would be so emotional and would draw even closer bonds with so many of you. We'll be forever grateful to each of you.

A special thanks to our fantastic editors at Unbound, Martha Sprackland, Phil Connor and copyeditor Hayley Shepherd, for their encouragement, enthusiasm, incisive comments and attention to detail which pushed us to truly polish our manuscript; and to our co-editor Charlotte Willis, who helped us bring together our manuscript before submitting it to Unbound. We're also deeply grateful to Mark Ecob for designing the striking cover and to the brilliant Unbound design and production teams for making this book a beautiful thing.

Some of our work first appeared on the webzine *Ecorazzi*, in one form or another. We thank *Ecorazzi* for publishing our work and for allowing us to present it to you in this book.

Whenever possible and when referring to people or animals, we use the gender neutral *they* because it's time we do so.

With deepest gratitude,
Emi & Eva
Spring 2021

List of Essays by Author

Joint: What Would Be the Answer in a Human Context?

Emilia A. Leese: Introduction; What Does It Mean to Be Vegan?; A Framework for Analysing Animal Issues; Serves Them Right!; Our Journey and Advocacy; Why Did I Go Vegan in My Forties?; The Rocky Road to My Partner Going Vegan; Honey Isn't Ours; If You Believe in Social Justice, You Believe in Veganism; Veganism and Poverty: Reconcilable and Intersectional; Exploitation and the Patriarchy; The Mechanisms of -Isms Are the Same; A Vegan Experiment; Only Forty-Six Days; Body Count; Beyond Meat; A Wicked Good Opportunity; What About 'No-Kill' Eggs?; Size Doesn't Matter; The California Fur Ban: What Does It Actually Accomplish?; What the Experts Say; Zoonotic Diseases: Our Deal With the Devil; Environmental Science; Land Use; Are We So Different from Climate Change Deniers?; Takeaways; Practical Thought Experiments

Eva J. Charalambides: Vegan or Plant-Based?: Vegans Don't Need Capes; Vegansexualism; How Being Straight Edge Prepared Me for Veganism; Veganism and Yoga; Libby: An Argument for Rescuing Animals; Veganism as a Measure of Health; Disordered Eating in Veganism; Frugal Vegan

Endnotes

Chapter 1

1. Thanks to Leonard Cohen's 'Anthem' for the inspiration https://www.telegraph.co.uk/music/artists/the-best-leonard-cohen-lyrics/
2. For an interesting overview of Pythagoras' philosophy regarding animals, see Mary Ann Violin, 'Pythagoras – The First Animal Rights Philosopher', *Between the Species*, Summer 1990 https://pdfs.semanticscholar.org/34a7/c90afc401830e49fd ba0952dccb5173709ac.pdf
3. Maimonides, *The Guide for the Perplexed*, trans. Shlomo Pines, University of Chicago Press, Chicago, 1963, 3:12, 442. For a fuller discussion about Maimonides, see Jacob Ari Labendz and Shmuly Yanklowitz, eds., *Jewish Veganism and Vegetarianism: Studies and New Directions*, SUNY Press, New York, 2019, pp. 176–179
4. *Ibid.* 3:48, 599
5. Jeremy Bentham, *An Introduction to the Principles of Morals and Legislation*, Clarendon Press, Oxford, 1780 (new ed. 1823), p. 311
6. 'Any being that is sentient necessarily has an interest in life because sentience is a means to the end of continued existence. To say that a nonhuman is sentient but does not have an interest in continued existence and does not prefer, want, or desire to live is peculiar.' Gary L. Francione, *Animals as Persons: Essays on the Abolition of Animal Exploitation*, Columbia University Press, 2008, p. 144. See also Sam Earl, 'How should we feel about the feelings of the animals we eat? Acknowledging the sentience of other species requires us to be vegan', Open Democracy, 12 December 2017 https://www.opendemocracy.net/en/transformation/how-should-we-feel-about-feelings-of-animals-we-eat/

7. 'We are each of us the experiencing subject of a life, a conscious creature having an individual welfare that has importance to us whatever our usefulness to others. We want and prefer things, believe and feel things, recall and expect things. And all these dimensions of our life, including our pleasure and pain, our enjoyment and suffering, our satisfaction and frustration, our continued existence or our untimely death – all make a difference to the quality of our life as lived, as experienced, by us as individuals. As the same is true of those animals that concern us (the ones that are eaten and trapped, for example), they too must be viewed as the experiencing subjects of a life, with inherent value of their own.' Tom Regan, 'The Case for Animal Rights', in M. W. Fox & L. D. Mickley (eds.), *Advances in Animal Welfare Science*, Humane Society of the United States, Washington D.C., 1986, p. 186 https://animalstudiesrepository.org/acwp_awap/3/

8. The Vegan Society, 'Ripened by human determination', *70 years of the Vegan Society* https://www.vegansociety.com/sites/default/files/uploads/Ripened%20by%20human%20determination.pdf

9. A novel example of this is a recent change in law in South Africa for thirty-three wild animal species, including lions, cheetahs, rhinos and zebras, whose status has been changed from wild to farm animals so they may be bred and killed for human use. https://www.dailymaverick.co.za/article/2019-10-16-sa-reclassifies-33-wild-species-as-farm-animals/

10. Animal welfare laws and organisations aren't new. They've existed for almost 200 years and our use and slaughter of animals hasn't abated in the slightest. The world's first animal welfare laws and organisation were adopted and founded in Great Britain. The Society for the Prevention of Cruelty to Animals, or SPCA, was founded in 1824. In 1822, the British Parliament passed the Act to Prevent the Cruel and Improper Treatment of Cattle, and the Protection of Animals Act in 1911.

11. For an extensive analysis of property laws and animals, see the seminal work by Gary Francione, *Animals, Property and the Law*, Temple University Press, Philadelphia, 1995

12. FAO Animal Production and Health Paper, *Guidelines for slaughtering, meat cutting and further processing*, 'Variations in the Sensoric Quality of Meat', Food and Agriculture Organization of the

United Nations, Rome, 1991 http://www.fao.org/3/t0279e/
t0279e05.htm

13. Caroline Stocks, 'Slaughtering beef animals at 12 months is
most profitable, say scientists', *Farmers Weekly*, 12 April 2016
https://www.fwi.co.uk/livestock/slaughtering-beef-animals-
12-months-profitable-say-scientists

14. Food Safety and Inspection Service, 'National Chicken Council – Spreadsheet Showing Average Slaughter Age', United
States Department of Agriculture, Washington D.C. https://
www.fsis.usda.gov/wps/wcm/connect/d146f197-7140-439a-
bc1e-83356d3c4f69/Petition-NCC-Slaughter-Age-Chickens.
pdf?MOD=AJPERES

15. Lexy Lebsack, 'Death Threats & £2 Ponytails: What The Fake
Hair Trade Is Hiding', *Refinery 29*, 1 May 2019 https://www.
refinery29.com/en-gb/2018/06/201466/human-hair-
extensions-ethical-sourcing; Homa Khaleeli, 'The hair trade's
dirty secret', the *Guardian*, 28 October 2012 https://www.
theguardian.com/lifeandstyle/2012/oct/28/hair-extension-
global-trade-secrets; Kirstie Brewer, 'Untangling where your
hair extensions really come from', *BBC News*, 1 November 2016
https://www.bbc.co.uk/news/magazine-37781147

16. Maureen Dowd, 'E.R.', *The New York Times*, 4 July 1999 (book
review Blanche Wiesen Cook, *Eleanor Roosevelt Volume 2: 1933–
1938*, Viking, 1999) https://www.nytimes.com/1999/07/04/
books/er.html; see also https://www.fdrlibrary.org/documents/
356632/390886/Fall2009-rendxnine.pdf/5d3cd428-41a5-
40cf-8e51-c77a80c128bd

17. Thanks to American professor, author, journalist and political
theorist Corey Robin for his thoughtful social media posts. This,
in particular, made us reflect on wider implications: 'But as
Eleanor Roosevelt said, if you're going to compromise, compromise up. Make your imperfection serve a larger perfection,
not your own advancement.' https://www.facebook.com/
corey.robin1/posts/2090767424322301

18. Chimamanda Ngozi Adichie and Reni Eddo-Lodge, 'In Conversation', Royal Festival Hall, 10 March 2018. From Emilia
Leese's own notes from the event

19. Eva Charalambides, 'Campaigns against fur don't work and
they promote the use of other animal products like wool',
Ecorazzi, 10 February 2016 http://www.ecorazzi.com/2016/

02/10/campaigns-against-fur-dont-work-and-they-promote-the-use-of-other-animal-products-like-wool/

20. Erin Strecker, 'Watch Beyoncé Explain Her Vegan Diet Benefits on "GMA"', *Billboard*, 8 June 2015 https://www.billboard.com/articles/news/6590635/beyonce-vegan-diet-book-delivery-service

Chapter 2

1. Skye Vadas, 'Inside the World of "Vegansexualism" – the Vegans Who Only Date Other Vegans', *Vice*, 10 October 2016 https://www.vice.com/en_us/article/dpk3az/vegans-who-only-have-sex-with-vegans

2. Jeff Stryker, 'Vegansexuality', *The New York Times*, 9 December 2007 https://www.nytimes.com/2007/12/09/magazine/09vegansexuality.html?_r=0

3. Eva Charalambides, 'If veganism is a moral choice why do vegans date non-vegans?', *Ecorazzi*, 17 March 2016 http://www.ecorazzi.com/2016/03/17/if-veganism-is-a-moral-choice-why-do-vegans-date-non-vegans/

4. What is straight edge? http://www.straightedge.com/whatissxe.html

5. Terianne O'Hara and Evan Decamp, both always in my heart.

6. Carol J. Adams, *The Sexual Politics of Meat: a feminist-vegetarian critical theory*. Continuum, New York, 1990.

7. William J. D. Doran, 'The Eight Limbs, The Core of Yoga' http://www.expressionsofspirit.com/yoga/eight-limbs.htm

8. *Lokah Samastah Sukhino Bhavantu* https://jivamuktiyoga.com/fotm/lokah-samastah-sukhino-bhavantu/

9. Sarah McLachlan animal cruelty video https://www.youtube.com/watch?v=9gspElvIyvc

10. Before going vegan, Emilia took a beekeeping course where this collateral damage was discussed as an acceptable risk.

11. Charlotte Willis and Elena Orde, 'Honey: The not so sweet reality behind why honey isn't vegan', *Vegan Food and Living*, 4 July 2016 https://www.veganfoodandliving.com/honey-not-so-sweet/

12. For example, Plant Based Artisan's Vegan Honea https://plantbasedartisan.com, or Beatnik Bees, https://beatnikbees.co.uk

13. Emily Cassel, '"Natural" Sugars Are Not Better for You Than Regular Sugar', *Vice*, 4 February 2019 https://www.vice.com/en_uk/article/bjeqa4/natural-sugars-are-not-better-for-you-than-regular-sugar

14. A review of a variety of studies involving honey for medicinal purposes show there's little to no good evidence for or against using honey and there are plenty of alternatives readily available https://www.cochrane.org/search/site/honey

Chapter 3

1. Benjamin MacEllen https://www.facebook.com/photo.php?fbid=10153927862727017&set=a.230725967016&type=3&theater

2. Food Empowerment Project, 'Factory Farm Workers' https://foodispower.org/human-labor-slavery/factory-farm-workers/; see also, Constantine Spyrou, 'The Shrimp Industry's Awful Issue of Slave Labor Continues To Plague It Today', *Food Beast*, 23 January 2018 https://www.foodbeast.com/news/shrimp-industry-slavery-2018/; and see, Lisa M. Keefe, 'What Would You Do?', *Meating Place*, 7 August 2019 https://outline.com/T9zZrf (https://www.meatingplace.com/Industry/Blogs/Details/86918); and also Michel Martin, 'ICE Raids Hit Poultry Processing Plants That Rely On Latino Immigrant Labor', *National Public Radio*, 10 August 2019 https://www.npr.org/2019/08/10/750172206/ice-raids-hit-poultry-processing-plants-that-rely-on-latino-immigrant-labor; and see, Michael Grabell and Bernice Yeung, 'Emails show the meatpacking industry drafted an executive order to keep plants open', *ProPublica*, 14 September 2020 https://www.propublica.org/article/emails-show-the-meatpacking-industry-drafted-an-executive-order-to-keep-plants-open

3. For extensive and current discussion of farm workers' exploitation see: Mica Rosenberg, Kristina Cooke, 'Allegations of labor abuses dogged Mississippi plant years before immigration raids', *Reuters*, 9 August 2019, https://www.reuters.com/article/us-usa-immigration-koch-foods/allegations-of-labor-abuses-dogged-mississippi-plant-years-before-immigration-raids-idUSKCN1UZ1OV; see also Policy Department for Citizens' Rights and Constitutional Affairs, *The vulnerability to exploitation of women migrant workers in agriculture in the EU: the need for a Human Rights and Gender based approach*, Directorate General for

Internal Policies of the Union, May 2018, http://www.europarl. europa.eu/RegData/etudes/STUD/2018/604966/ IPOL_STU(2018)604966_EN.pdf; and ANSA, 'Italian food system exploits migrant farm workers – UN", *InfoMigrants*, 4 February 2020, https://www.infomigrants.net/en/post/22540/ italian-food-system-exploits-migrant-farm-workers-un; and Kieran Guilbert, 'Europe struggling to "catch" bad bosses who enslave migrant workers', *Reuters*, 5 September 2018, https:// www.reuters.com/article/us-europe-slavery-migrants/europe- struggling-to-catch-bad-bosses-who-enslave-migrant-workers- idUSKCN1LLoLA; and European Union Agency for Funda- mental Rights, *Protecting migrant workers from exploitation in the EU: workers' perspectives*, Publications Office of the European Union, Luxembourg, 2019, https://fra.europa.eu/sites/default/files/ fra_uploads/fra-2019-severe-labour-exploitation-workers-per- spectives_en.pdf; and Philip Case, 'Shocking extent of modern slavery in agriculture revealed', *Farmers Weekly*, 18 May 2018, https://www.fwi.co.uk/news/shocking-extent-of-modern- slavery-in-agriculture-revealed; and Human Rights Watch, *Blood, Sweat, and Fear: Workers' Rights in U.S. Meat and Poultry Plants*, 24 January 2005, https://www.hrw.org/report/2005/ 01/24/blood-sweat-and-fear/workers-rights-us-meat-and- poultry-plants ; and Erica Battaglia, 'Donne braccianti, l'inch- iesta che finisce sulle nostre tavole', Vita a Sud, 21 maggio 2018 http://www.vita.it/it/interview/2018/05/21/oro-rosso- fragole-pomodori-ed-esame-di-coscienza-a-tavola/180/? fbclid=IwAR0_s8teROszpGqo7yWpHEeI5sAqcJNvBtgy- 1jV3aDPpaUQu936myM3dNf4 discussing the two years' work of Stefania Prandi among the migrant agricultural workers and pickers, particularly women in Italy, Spain and Morocco; see also, 'Tomatoes' Journey Around the World' a video about China's tomato pickers https://www.facebookcom/ 18323956178779o/videos/1590474497730949; and with respect to the USA, see the work of Food Empowerment Project at https://foodispower.org

4. Hannah Ritchie, 'Which countries eat the most meat?', *BBC*, 4 February 2019 https://www.bbc.co.uk/news/health47057341

5. Colonisation, classism, other forms of cultural supremacy and cultural and economic shifts have played a significant role in the acculturation of foods. See for example, Dr. Linda Alvarez

'Colonization, food, and the practice of eating', *The Food Empowerment Project* https://foodispower.org/our-food-choices/colonization-food-and-the-practice-of-eating/; see also Ayoola Oladipupo 'Neocolonization on a plate, with a soda to go', *Africa Is a Country*, 28 October 2020 https://africasacountry.com/2020/10/neocolonization-on-a-plate-with-a-soda-to-go; and see Buzina R, Suboticanec K, Sarić M, 'Diet patterns and health problems: diet in southern Europe', *Ann Nutr Metab*, 1991;35 Suppl 1:32-40. doi: 10.1159/000177676. PMID: 1888126 https://pubmed.ncbi.nlm.nih.gov/1888126/; and see Trichopoulou A., 'Mediterranean diet: the past and the present.' *Nutrition, metabolism, and cardiovascular diseases*, 2001, 11(4 Suppl), 1–4 https://pubmed.ncbi.nlm.nih.gov/11894739/

6. Union of Concerned Scientists, 'The Devastating Consequences of Unequal Food Access – The Role of Race and Income in Diabetes', April 2016 https://www.ucsusa.org/sites/default/files/attach/2016/04/ucs-race-income-diabetes-2016.pdf; see also Allan S. Noonan, Hector Eduardo Velasco-Mondragon and Fernando A. Wagner, 'Improving the health of African Americans in the USA: an overdue opportunity for social justice', *Public Health Reviews*, 3 October 2016 https://publichealthreviews.biomedcentral.com/articles/10.1186/s40985-016-0025-4; and see Anna Brones, 'Food apartheid: the root of the problem with America's groceries', the *Guardian*, 15 May 2018 https://www.theguardian.com/society/2018/may/15/food-apartheid-food-deserts-racism-inequality-america-karen-washington-interview; and see National Academy of Sciences, Baciu A, Negussie Y, Geller A, et al., editors, *Communities in Action: Pathways to Health Equity*, 'The State of Health Disparities in the United States', 2017 https://www.ncbi.nlm.nih.gov/books/NBK425844/; and see REACH Community Health Project, 'Mapping Exercise of Third Sector Food & Health initiatives with Minority Ethnic Communities in Scotland', March 2010 https://www.communityfoodandhealth.org.uk/wp-content/uploads/2012/02/cfhs-reach-mapping-exercise-minority-ethnic-communities.pdf

7. Anna Brones, 'Karen Washington: It's Not a Food Desert, It's Food Apartheid' *Guernica*, 7 May 2018 https://www.guernicamag.com/karen-washington-its-not-a-food-desert-its-food-apartheid/

8. Sarah Kliff, 'Do food deserts matter? Do they even exist?', *Washington Post*, 18 April 2012 https://www.washingtonpost.

com/blogs/ezra-klein/post/do-food-deserts-matter-do-they-even-exist/2012/04/18/gIQA1B56QT_blog.html

9. Richard Florida, 'It's Not the Food Deserts: It's the Inequality', *Citylab*, 18 January 2018 https://www.citylab.com/equity/2018/01/its-not-the-food-deserts-its-the-inequality/550793/; see also Patrick Butler, 'More than a million UK residents live in "food deserts", says study', the *Guardian*, 12 October 2018 https://www.theguardian.com/society/2018/oct/12/more-than-a-million-uk-residents-live-in-food-deserts-says-study; and see, Nigel Roberts, 'New Generation of Black-Led Co-ops Want to End Food Insecurity', *The Root*, 19 December 2019 https://www.theroot.com/new-generation-of-black-led-co-ops-want-to-end-food-ins-1840411111

10. For a good story on Latinx people embracing vegan Mexican food, see Gustavo Arellano, 'Carne Asada, Hold The Meat: Why Latinos Are Embracing Vegan-Mexican Cuisine', *The Salt*, National Public Radio, 19 July 2018 https://www.npr.org/sections/thesalt/2018/07/19/629629261/carne-asada-hold-the-meat-why-latinos-are-embracing-vegan-mexican-cuisine

11. Daniel A. Sumner, 'Agricultural Subsidy Programs', *The Library of Economics and Liberty* https://www.econlib.org/library/Enc/AgriculturalSubsidyPrograms.html; see also: 'Should governments subsidise the meat and dairy industries?' *Medium*, 19 December 2016 https://medium.com/@laletur/should-governments-subsidy-the-meat-and-dairy-industries-6ce59e68d26; and also Andrew Wasley and Alexandra Heal, 'Revealed: US-style industrial farms receive millions in subsidies', the *Guardian*, 28 December 2018 https://www.theguardian.com/environment/2018/dec/28/revealed-industrial-scale-farms-receive-millions-in-subsidies; and also, Elle Hunt, '*Meatonomics* author says government working with meat and dairy industry to boost consumption', the *Guardian*, 6 May 2017 https://www.theguardian.com/science/2017/may/06/meatonomics-author-says-government-working-with-meat-and-dairy-industry-to-boost-consumption; and also Tom Levitt, 'EU ignoring climate crisis with livestock farm subsidies, campaigners warn', the *Guardian*, 22 May 2019 https://www.theguardian.com/environment/2019/may/22/eu-ignoring-climate-crisis-with-livestock-farm-subsidies-campaigners-warn; and also Trevor J. Smith, 'Corn, Cows, and Climate Change: How

Federal Agricultural Subsidies Enable Factory Farming and Exacerbate U.S. Greenhouse Gas Emissions', *Washington Journal of Environmental Law & Policy*, Volume 9, Issue 1, 2019 https://digitalcommons.law.uw.edu/wjelp/vol9/iss1/3

12. Maimonides, *The Guide for the Perplexed*, trans. Shlomo Pines, University of Chicago Press, Chicago, 1963, 3:48, p. 599. For a fuller discussion about Maimonides, see Jacob Ari Labendz and Shmuly Yanklowitz, eds., *Jewish Veganism and Vegetarianism: Studies and New Directions*, SUNY Press, New York, 2019, pp. 176–179

Chapter 4

1. Brian Kateman, 'Swapping Out Red Meat For Poultry Or Seafood? You May Be Causing More Harm', *Forbes*, 15 October 2019 https://www.forbes.com/sites/brankateman/2019/10/15/swapping-out-red-meat-for-poultry-or-seafood-you-may-be-causing-more-harm/?fbclid=IwAR3dKzh-KNUm-6Kg1gkvROieX20Sbug0JEnjp8R0FVC7y-SvikdIz6zXHgI#639d2a7f5d56

2. Professor Al Slocum was a legend and shall be missed. https://law.rutgers.edu/news/remembering-professor-al-slocum-champion-underclass

3. Hannah Ritchie and Max Roser, 'Meat and Dairy Production – Meat and Seafood Production & Consumption', *Our World in Data*, first published in August 2017, last revision in November 2019 https://ourworldindata.org/meat-and-seafood-production-consumption#number-of-animals-slaughtered-for-meat

4. Michelle Perret, 'HSBC report forecasts 17% rise in meat production', *Global Meat News*, 20 November 2015 https://www.globalmeatnews.com/Article/2015/11/20/HSBC-report-forecasts-17-rise-in-meat-production

5. *Ibid.*

6. 'Ruling the roost', *The Economist*, 15 January 2019

7. OECD-FAO Agricultural Outlook 2016–2025, 'Meat – Projection Highlights', OECD Publishing, Paris, p. 107 http://www.fao.org/3/a-BO100e.pdf

8. Hannah Ritchie and Max Roser, 'Meat and Dairy Production – Per Capita Meat Consumption – Which countries eat the most meat?', *Our World in Data*, first published in August 2017, last revision in November 2019 https://ourworldindata.org/

meat-and-seafood-production-consumption#per-capita-trends-in-meat-consumption

9. Skye Gould and Lauren F. Friedman, 'Here's how American meat-eating habits have changed over time', *Business Insider*, 6 December 2015 https://www.businessinsider.com/how-american-meat-eating-habits-have-changed-2015-12?r= US&IR=T

10. Rob Cook, 'World Beef Production: Ranking of Countries', *Beef2Live*, 23 January 2020 https://beef2live.com/story-world-beef-production-ranking-countries-0-106885

11. 'American beef consumption up as meat prices decline', *Fox News*, updated 27 November 2016 https://www.foxnews.com/food-drink/american-beef-consumption-up-as-meat-prices-decline

12. Amy Unglesbee, 'Livestock & Poultry Outlook – Another Record Year for Meat Production Forecast for 2019', *Progressive Farmer*, 22 February 2019 https://www.dtnpf.com/agriculture/web/ag/news/article/2019/02/22/another-record-year-meat-production

13. Alice Mitchell, 'CME: US Meat Production Expected to Hit Record', *The Pig Site*, 22 October 2015 https://thepigsite.com/news/2015/10/cme-us-meat-production-expected-to-hit-record-1

14. 'Meat consumption is changing but it's not because of vegans', *Food Matters Live*, 21 March 2019 https://www.foodmatterslive.com/news-and-comment/news/meat-consumption-is-changing; see also, Stephen Leahy, 'Choosing chicken over beef cuts our carbon footprints a surprising amount', *National Geographic*, 11 June 2019 https://www.nationalgeographic.co.uk/environment/2019/06/choosing-chicken-over-beef-cuts-our-carbon-footprints-surprising-amount; and Roni A Neff, Danielle Edwards, Anne Palmer, Rebecca Ramsing, Allison Righter, and Julia Wolfson, 'Reducing meat consumption in the USA: a nationally representative survey of attitudes and behaviours', *Public Health Nutrition*, Cambridge University Press, 26 March 2018 https://www.ncbi.nlm.nih.gov/pmc/articles/PMC6088533/; and also 'Food consumption – animal based protein', *European Environment Agency*, published 29 Nov 2018, last modified 26 Nov 2019 https://www.eea.europa.eu/airs/2018/resource-efficiency-and-low-carbon-economy/food-consumption-animal-based

15. Betsy Jibben, 'China Reaches for More U.S. Pork', *Ag Web*, 15 June 2016 https://www.agweb.com/mobile/article/china-reaches-for-more-us-pork-naa-betsy-jibben/

16. Theopolis Waters, 'Record U.S. pork stocks spell affordable Easter hams, robust bacon demand', *Reuters*, 24 February 2016 https://www.reuters.com/article/usa-pork-storage/record-u-s-pork-stocks-spell-affordable-easter-hams-robust-bacon-demand-idUSL2N1622Oo

17. Hannah Ritchie and Max Roser, 'Meat and Dairy Production – Milk Production Across the World', *Our World in Data*, first published in August 2017, last revision in November 2019 https://ourworldindata.org/meat-and-seafood-production-consumption#milk-production-across-the-world

18. National Agricultural Statistics Service (NASS), Agricultural Statistics Board, United States Department of Agriculture (USDA), 'Milk Production', 21 October 2019 https://downloads.usda.library.cornell.edu/usda-esmis/files/h989r321c/7h14b4021/8p58pt248/mkpr1019.pdf

19. NASS, 'Milk Cows, 2009–2018, United States', USDA, 12 March 2019 https://www.nass.usda.gov/Charts_and_Maps/Milk_Production_and_Milk_Cows/milkcows.php

20. NASS 'Milk-cow numbers turn higher and output per cow continues to grow', USDA, 15 April 2016 https://www.ers.usda.gov/data-products/chart-gallery/gallery/chart-detail/?chartId=78889

21. NASS 'Milk: Production per cow, 2009–2018', USDA, 12 March 2019 https://www.nass.usda.gov/Charts_and_Maps/Milk_Production_and_Milk_Cows/cowrates.php

22. 'Milk produced per cow in the United States from 1999 to 2018 (in pounds)', *Statista*, March 2019 https://www.statista.com/statistics/194935/quantity-of-milk-produced-per-cow-in-the-us-since-1999/

23. *Ibid.*

24. NASS, 'Milk-cow numbers turn higher and output per cow continues to grow', USDA, 15 April 2016 https://www.ers.usda.gov/data-products/chart-gallery/gallery/chart-detail/?chartId=78889

25. John Geuss, 'Why does the US continue to drink less milk?', *DairyReporter.com*, 26 November 2013 https://www.dairyreporter.

com/Article/2013/11/26/Why-does-the-US-continue-to-drink-less-milk

26. Emily Moon, 'What Will the U.S. Government Do With 1.4 Billion Pounds of Cheese?', *Pacific Standard*, 10 January 2019 https://psmag.com/economics/what-will-the-us-government-do-with-1-4-billion-pounds-of-cheese

27. *Ibid.*

28. Anna-Lisa Laca, 'Walmart Opens Indiana Milk Plant', *Farm-Journal's Milk*, 13 June 2018 https://www.milkbusiness.com/article/walmart-opens-indiana-milk-plant

29. Jeremy Gerrard, 'Walmart to build Indiana milk process-ing plant', *Food Engineering*, 18 March 2016 https://www.food-engineeringmag.com/articles/95430-walmart-to-build-indiana-milk-processing-plant

30. Donna Boss, 'Retailers Pressure Dairy Industry with New Plants', *Supermarket News*, 1 November 2017 https://www.supermarketnews.com/dairy/retailers-pressure-dairy-industry-new-plants

31. Micah Maidenberg and Jaewon Kang, 'Cereal Makers Try Again to Jump-Start Stale Sales', *The Wall Street Journal*, 20 August 2019 https://www.wsj.com/articles/cereal-makers-try-again-to-jump-start-stale-sales-11566293404; see also Associated Press, 'Another major US dairy, Borden, seeks bankruptcy protection', *New York Post*, 6 January 2020 https://nypost.com/2020/01/06/another-major-us-dairy-borden-seeks-bankruptcy-protection/

32. Lillianna Byington, 'How Dean Foods' bankruptcy is a "warn-ing sign" to the milk industry', *Food Dive*, 21 November 2019 https://www.fooddive.com/news/how-dean-foods-bankruptcy-is-a-warning-sign-to-the-milk-industry/567486/

33. Amelia Lucas, '5 charts that show how milk sales changed and made it tough for Dean Foods to avert bankruptcy', *CNBC*, 13 November 2019 https://www.cnbc.com/2019/11/13/5-charts-that-show-how-milk-sales-have-changed.html

34. *Ibid*; see also Rachel Siegel, 'Borden Dairy becomes second major milk producer to file for bankruptcy in two months', the *Washington Post*, 6 January 2020 https://www.washingtonpost.com/business/2020/01/06/borden-dairy-files-bankruptcy-amid-debt-load-headwinds-facing-milk-producers/; and see Borden Dairy's bankruptcy court docket https://s.wsj.net/public/

resources/documents/borden_dairy_cfo_declaration.pdf?-mod=article_inline

35. *Ibid.*

36. Tonya Garcia, 'Dean Foods files for bankruptcy as oat milk and other alternatives gain popularity', *Market Watch*, 12 November 2019 https://www.marketwatch.com/story/dean-foods-files-for-bankruptcy-as-oat-milk-and-other-alternatives-gain-popularity-2019-11-12; see also Louis Biscotti, 'Why Borden Dairy's Bankruptcy Filing Might Be A Glass-Half-Full Scenario', *Forbes*, 8 January 2020 https://www.forbes.com/sites/louisbiscotti/2020/01/08/borden-heads-into-bankruptcy-charts-new-course/#47c492dc1778; see also 'Borden files for Chapter 11 bankruptcy protection', *Dallas Business Journal*, 5 January 2020 https://www.bizjournals.com/dallas/news/2020/01/05/borden-chapter-11-bankruptcy.html; see also Jesse Colombo, 'Here's why more American farms are going bankrupt', *Forbes*, 29 November 2018 https://www.forbes.com/sites/jessecolombo/2018/11/29/heres-why-more-american-farms-are-going-bankrupt/#2f312a8f65a7

37. Myra P. Saefong, 'Why farm bankruptcies have climbed, even with milk and cheese prices up 40% this year', *Market Watch*, 15 November 2019 https://www.marketwatch.com/story/why-farm-bankruptcies-have-climbed-even-with-milk-and-cheese-prices-up-40-this-year-2019-11-15; see also Byington, 'How Dean Foods' bankruptcy is a "warning sign" to the milk industry'

38. Oliver Milman and Stuart Leavenworth, 'China's plan to cut meat consumption by 50% cheered by climate campaigners', the *Guardian*, 20 June 2016 https://www.theguardian.comworld/2016/jun/20/chinas-meat-consumption-climate-change

39. 'Less Meat, Less Heat: Behind the Scenes with James Cameron & Arnold Schwarzenegger', https://vimeo.com/169913909; see also Catherine Shoard, 'Arnold Schwarzenegger and James Cameron urge people to eat less meat', the *Guardian*, 23 June 2016 https://www.theguardian.com/film/2016/jun/23/arnold-schwarzenegger-james-cameron-eat-less-meat-china

40. Rob Cook, 'World Beef Production: Ranking of Countries', *Beef2Live*, 23 January 2020 https://beef2live.com/story-world-beef-production-ranking-countries-0-106885

41. Mark Godfrey, 'China tipped for beef boom', *Global Meat News*, 15 June 2016 https://www.globalmeatnews.com/Article/

2016/06/15/China-tipped-for-beef-boom; see also Oscar Rousseau, 'China's Maling enters beef industry', *Global Meat News*, 2 June 2016 https://www.globalmeatnews.com/Article/2016/06/02/China-s-Maling-enters-beef-industry

42. Felicity Lawrence, 'Can the world quench China's bottomless thirst for milk?', the *Guardian*, 29 March 2019 https://www.theguardian.com/environment/2019/mar/29/can-the-world-quench-chinas-bottomless-thirst-for-milk?CMP=Share_iOSApp_Other

43. Mark Godfrey, 'China's meat firms invest in pig herd growth', *Global Meat News*, 22 February 2016 https://www.globalmeatnews.com/Article/2016/02/22/China-s-meat-firms-invest-in-pig-herd-growth

44. Oscar Rousseau, 'China's pork imports booming', *Global Meat News*, 29 April 2016 https://www.globalmeatnews.com/Article/2016/04/29/China-s-pork-imports-booming

45. Tom Polansek, 'Locked out of China, U.S. pork producers sniff out new buyers', *Reuters*, 2 July 2019 https://www.reuters.com/article/us-usa-trade-china-hogs-insight/locked-out-of-china-u-s-pork-producers-sniff-out-new-buyers-idUSKCN1TX0GV

46. Keith Good, 'African Swine Fever Impacting Chinese Protein Markets and U.S. Pork Exports', *Farm Policy News*, 23 July 2019 https://farmpolicynews.illinois.edu/2019/07/african-swine-fever-impacting-chinese-protein-markets-and-u-s-pork-exports/

47. 'Germany overtakes Spain as the largest supplier of pork in China', *Euromeat News*, 11 February 2019 http://euromeatnews.com/Article-Germany-overtakes-Spain-as-the-largest-supplier-of-pork-in-China/2562

48. Monica Liau, 'Chinese People Love Pork so Much, the Government Has a National Pork Reserve', *Culture Trip*, 29 January 2018 https://theculturetrip.com/asia/china/articles/chinese-people-love-pork-much-government-national-pork-reserve/

49. Aaron McDonald, 'Beijing releases reserve pork', *Global Meat News*, 10 May 2016 https://www.globalmeatnews.com/Article/2016/05/11/Beijing-releases-reserve-pork

50. Jenny Splitter, 'African Swine Fever Continues To Devastate China's Pork Supply, But U.S. Farmers Are Unlikely To Fill The Need', *Forbes*, 6 August 2019 https://www.forbes.com/sites/jennysplitter/2019/08/06/china-might-need-more-pork-but-us-farmers-are-unlikely-to-benefit/

51. Susan Kelly, 'USTR details China trade deal impact on meat, poultry', *Meatingplace*, 16 January 2020 https://www.meatingplace.com/Industry/News/Details/89784

52. Chris Scott, 'China buys $418M worth of U.S. chicken, '21 outlook improves', *Meatingplace*, 10 November 2020 https://www.meatingplace.com/Industry/News/Details/95480

53. *Ibid.*

54. Economic Research Service, 'China's Foreign Agriculture Investments', United States Department of Agriculture, April 2018 https://www.ers.usda.gov/publications/pub-details/?pubid=88571

55. Oscar Rousseau, 'Red meat predicted to post growth of £8.1bn', *Global Meat News*, 14 December 2015 https://www.globalmeatnews.com/Article/2015/12/14/Red-meat-predicted-to-post-growth-of-8.1bn

56. 'Q&A on the carcinogenicity of the consumption of red meat and processed meat', World Health Organization, October 2015 https://www.who.int/features/qa/cancer-red-meat/en/

57. Oscar Rousseau, 'Red meat predicted to post growth of £8.1bn', *Global Meat News*, 14 December 2015 https://www.globalmeatnews.com/Article/2015/12/14/Red-meat-predicted-to-post-growth-of-8.1bn

58. 'UK red meat production up in 2015', *FarmingUK*, 15 February 2016 https://www.farminguk.com/News/UK-red-meat-production-up-in-2015_38673.html

59. *Ibid.*

60. 'UK beef production on the rise', Agriculture and Horticulture Development Board, 23 May 2018 http://beefandlamb.ahdb.org.uk/market-intelligence-news/uk-beef-production-rise/

61. 'Extreme weather of 2018 makes its mark on red meat production', *FarmingUK*, 29 October 2018 https://www.farminguk.com/news/extreme-weather-of-2018-makes-its-mark-on-red-meat-production_50590.html

62. Laura Parnaby, 'UK slaughterhouses killing more animals despite growth of veganism', *Independent*, 27 January 2020 https://www.independent.co.uk/news/uk/home-news/slaughterhouse-kill-animals-meat-vegan-diet-plant-based-a9303386.html

63. 'Historical statistics notices on the number of cattle, sheep and pigs slaughtered in the UK, 2019', Department for Environ-

ment, Food & Rural Affairs, 16 January 2020 https://www.gov.uk/government/statistics/historical-statistics-notices-on-the-number-of-cattle-sheep-and-pigs-slaughtered-in-the-uk-2019

64. Claire Colley and Andrew Wasley, 'Industrial-sized pig and chicken farming continuing to rise in UK', the *Guardian*, 7 April 2020 https://www.theguardian.com/environment/2020/apr/07/industrial-sized-pig-and-chicken-farming-continuing-to-rise-in-uk

65. *Ibid.*

66. Michelle Perrett, 'UK beef sales continue to fall as consumers make lifestyle choices', *Food Manufacture*, 3 February 2020 https://www.foodmanufacture.co.uk/Article/2020/02/03/Beef-sales-continue-to-fall

67. *Ibid.*

68. Darren Boyle, 'Craze for vegan diets makes meat suffer biggest fall in supermarket sales above any other type of food and drink as Veganuary begins', *Mail Online*, 1 January 2020 https://www.dailymail.co.uk/news/article-7842663/Craze-vegan-diets-makes-meat-suffers-biggest-fall-supermarket-sales.html?ito=facebook_share_article-top; see also Ben Webster, 'Sales of beef and pork plunge as Britons choose vegan diet', *The Times*, 2 January 2020 https://www.thetimes.co.uk/article/red-meat-sales-hit-as-800-000-people-go-vegetarian-kpz2k3xnz?fbclid=IwAR1iKFeM6XhcSi9stzioFaccl6IcoFR9MAGUTUDJy3E4r34XRYdt5kPbIXM

69. Perrett, 'UK beef sales continue to fall . . .'

70. Philip Clarke, 'Egg sales heading for a record year', *Farmers Weekly*, 4 November 2015 https://www.fwi.co.uk/livestock/poultry/eggs/egg-sales-heading-for-a-record-year; see also FW reporter, 'Outlook 2020: Welfare and price issues split poultry sector', *Farmers Weekly*, 29 December 2019 https://www.fwi.co.uk/business/markets-and-trends/meat-prices/outlook-2020-welfare-and-price-issues-split-poultry-sector

71. Rebecca Smithers, 'Shoppers shell out on 6bn eggs as flexitarians help drive UK revival', the *Guardian*, 26 February 2020 https://www.theguardian.com/food/2020/feb/26/shoppers-shell-out-billions-eggs-flexitarians-uk-revival?CMP=share_btn_fb

72. 'Britain ate an EXTRA 275m eggs last year as they come back into fashion after health scares', *Mirror*, 29 January 2016 https://

www.mirror.co.uk/news/uk-news/britain-ate-extra-275m-eggs-7271058; see also Rebecca Smithers, the *Guardian*, 26 February 2020 https://www.theguardian.com/food/2020/feb/26/shoppers-shell-out-billions-eggs-flexitarians-uk-revival?CMP=share_btn_fb

73. 'Food consumption – animal based protein', *European Environment Agency*, published 29 November 2018, last modified 26 Nov 2019 https://www.eea.europa.eu/airs/2018/resource-efficiency-and-low-carbon-economy/food-consumption-animal-based; see also Brian Kateman, 'Swapping Out Red Meat For Poultry Or Seafood? You May Be Causing More Harm', *Forbes*, 15 October 2019 https://www.forbes.com/sites/briankateman/2019/10/15/swapping-out-red-meat-for-poultry-or-seafood-you-may-be-causing-more-harm/?fbclid=IwAR3dKzh-KNUm-6Kg1gkvROieX2oSbug0JEnjp8R0FVC7y-SvikdIz6zXHgI#639d2a7f5d56

74. FW reporter, 'Outlook 2020: Welfare and price issues split poultry sector', *Farmers Weekly*, 29 December 2019 https://www.fwi.co.uk/business/markets-and-trends/meat-prices/outlook-2020-welfare-and-price-issues-split-poultry-sector

75. Rob Cook, 'World Beef Production: Ranking Of Countries', *Beef2Live*, 23 January 2020 https://beef2live.com/story-world-beef-production-ranking-countries-0-106885

76. 'EU pig meat consumption rising, says [*sic*] new figures', *FarmingUK*, 30 March 2016 https://www.farminguk.com/News/EU-pig-meat-consumption-rising-says-new-figures_39206.html

77. Hannah Ritchie and Max Roser, 'Meat and Dairy Production – Milk Production Across the World', *Our World in Data*, first published in August 2017, last revision in November 2019 https://ourworldindata.org/meat-and-seafood-production-consumption#milk-production-across-the-world

78. 'The Dairy & Milk Processing Market in India, 2018–2019 & 2023', *Business Wire*, 22 March 2019 https://www.businesswire.com/news/home/20190322005336/en/Dairy-Milk-Processing-Market-India-2018-2019-2023

79. 'Dairy Industry in India 2020 Edition: Market Size, Growth, Prices, Segments, Cooperatives, Private Dairies, Procurement and Distribution', IMARC https://www.imarcgroup.com/dairy-industry-in-india

80. Rob Cook, 'World Beef Exports: Ranking of Countries',

Beef2Live, 2 February 2020 https://beef2live.com/story-world-beef-exports-ranking-countries-0-106903

81. Rob Cook, 'World Beef Production: Ranking of Countries', *Beef2Live*, 23 January 2020 https://beef2live.com/story-world-beef-production-ranking-countries-0-106885

82. Yamini Narayanan, '"Cow Is a Mother, Mothers Can Do Anything for Their Children!" Gaushalas as Landscapes of Anthropatriarchy and Hindu Patriarchy', 27 February 2019 https://onlinelibrary.wiley.com/doi/abs/10.1111/hypa.12460?af=R

83. Sagar Malviya and Ratna Bhushan, 'Chicken consumption growing at 12%, making India one of the fastest growing markets', *Economic Times*, 10 October 2015 https://economictimes.indiatimes.com/industry/cons-products/food/chicken-consumption-growing-at-12-making-india-one-of-the-fastest-growing-markets/articleshow/49295260.cms?from=mdr

84. Rob Cook, 'World Beef Production: Ranking of Countries', *Beef2Live*, 23 January 2020 https://beef2live.com/story-world-beef-production-ranking-countries-0-106885

85. Ashley Williams, 'Brazil closes 2018 with largest-ever beef volume exports', *Global Meat News*, 22 January 2019 https://www.globalmeatnews.com/Article/2019/01/22/Largest-ever-beef-exports-by-volume-for-Brazil

86. Tom Polansek, 'U.S. bans fresh Brazil beef imports over safety concerns', *Reuters*, 22 June 2017 https://it.reuters.com/article/idUSKBN19D2VE

87. Daniel Workman, 'Soya Beans Exports by Country', *World's Top Exports*, 26 September 2019 http://www.worldstopexports.com/soya-beans-exports-country/

88. Daniel Ren, 'The US–China trade war has been a boon for Brazil's soybean farmers. But can they keep up with Chinese demand?', *South China Morning Post*, 17 May 2019 https://www.scmp.com/business/companies/article/3010480/us-china-trade-war-has-been-boon-brazils-soybean-farmers-can

89. U.S. Soybean Export Council, *How the Global Oilseed and Grain Trade Works*, 2008 https://ussec.org/wp-content/uploads/2015/10/How-the-Global-Oilseed-and-Grain-Trade-Works.pdf at p. 6; see also, NC Soybean Producer Association, 'Uses of soybean' https://ncsoy.org/media-resources/uses-of-soybeans/; and see Kendra Wills, 'Where do all these soybeans go?', *Michigan State*

University, 8 October 2013 https://www.canr.msu.edu/news/where_do_all_these_soybeans_go; and see also, Hannah Ritchie, 'Soy', *Our World In Data* https://ourworldindata.org/soy?fbclid=IwAR3srYlorpdNcpeWdEVT6_YdpIU7TVWLlVGrQQEkoLzZd_eH-ZMU37inXSI

90. Soybean Export Council, *Global Oilseed and Grain Trade* https://ussec.org/wp-content/uploads/2015/10/How-the-Global-Oilseed-and-Grain-Trade-Works.pdf at p. 5; and see also, Hannah Ritchie, 'Soy', *Our World In Data* https://ourworldindata.org/soy?fbclid=IwAR3srYlorpdNcpeWdEVT6_YdpIU7T-VWLlVGrQQEkoLzZd_eH-ZMU37inXSI

91. Union of Concerned Scientists, 'Soybeans', 9 October 2015 https://www.ucsusa.org/global-warming/stop-deforestation/drivers-of-deforestation-2016-soybeans; see also Profundo Research and Advice, 'Soy Barometer 2014', Dutch Soy Coalition, September 2014 https://dn9ly4f9mxjxv.cloudfront.net/app/uploads/2017/03/07102143/141.105.120.208_dsc_wp-content_uploads_2014_04_Soy-Barometer2014.pdf; and see also, Hannah Ritchie, 'Soy', *Our World In Data* https://ourworldindata.org/soy?fbclid=IwAR3srYlorpdNcpeWdEVT6_YdpIU7TVWLlVGrQQEkoLzZd_eH-ZMU37inXSI

92. Chain Reaction Research, 'Deforestation in the Brazilian Soy Supply Chain: Market Access Risk from a Growing Share of Sourcing Commitments', 22 December 2017 https://chainreactionresearch.com/report/deforestation-in-the-brazilian-soy-supply-chain-market-access-risk-from-a-growing-share-of-sourcing-commitments/

93. Gro Intelligence, 'Brazilian Soybeans and the Amazon Rainforest', 6 September 2017 https://gro-intelligence.com/insights/articles/brazil-soybeans-amazon-rainforest

94. 'Brazil curbs soy farming deforestation in Amazon', *Reuters*, 10 January 2018 https://www.reuters.com/article/us-brazil-soy-amazon/brazil-curbs-soy-farming-deforestation-in-amazon-idUSKBN1EZ2BM

95. Zoe Sullivan, 'The Real Reason the Amazon Is On Fire', *Time*, 26 August 2019 https://time.com/5661162/why-the-amazon-is-on-fire/

96. Jake Spring, 'Soy boom devours Brazil's tropical savanna', *Reuters*, 28 August 2018 https://www.reuters.com/investigates/special-report/brazil-deforestation/

97. Niall McCarthy, 'Deforestation Helped Make Brazil The World's Top Soy Producer', *Forbes*, 27 August 2019 https://www.forbes.com/sites/niallmccarthy/2019/08/27/deforestation-helped-make-brazil-the-worlds-top-soy-producer-infographic/

98. Alexander Zaitchik, 'Rainforest on Fire – On the Front Lines of Bolsonaro's War on the Amazon, Brazil's Forest Communities Fight Against Climate Catastrophe', *The Intercept*, 6 July 2019 https://theintercept.com/2019/07/06/brazil-amazon-rainforest-indigenous-conservation-agribusiness-ranching/; see also Dom Phillips, 'Brazilian meat companies linked to farmer charged with 'massacre' in Amazon', the *Guardian*, 3 March 2020, https://www.theguardian.com/environment/2020/mar/03/brazilian-meat-companies-linked-to-farmer-charged-with-massacre-in-amazon

99. Oliver Milman, 'Scientists say halting deforestation "just as urgent" as reducing emissions', the *Guardian*, 4 October 2018 https://www.theguardian.com/environment/2018/oct/04/climate-change-deforestation-global-warming-report; see also, Zaitchik, 'Rainforest on Fire'

100. Grandview Research, 'Vegan Food Market Size Worth $24.06 Billion By 2025 | CAGR 9.6%', June 2019 https://www.grandviewresearch.com/press-release/global-vegan-food-market

101. Ellen Hammett, 'Veganism on the rise: How retailers are responding to the growing appetite for plant-based food', *Marketing Week*, 2 April 2019 https://www.marketingweek.com/retailers-vegan-plant-based-food/

102. Press Association, 'Almost one in four food products launched in UK in 2019 labelled vegan', the *Guardian*, 17 January 2020 https://www.theguardian.com/food/2020/jan/17/almost-one-in-four-food-products-launched-in-uk-in-2019-labelled-vegan

103 Justin McCarthy and Scott Dekoster, 'Four in 10 Americans Have Eaten Plant-Based Meats', *Gallup*, 28 January 2020 https://news.gallup.com/poll/282989/four-americans-eaten-plant-based-meats.aspx

104. Tyson Foods' website, SEC filings https://ir.tyson.com/sec-filings/default.aspx

105. Tyson Foods' website, What We Do https://www.tysonfoods.com/who-we-are/our-story/what-we-do

106. *Ibid.*

107. Beyond Meat, initial public offering document filed with the SEC https://www.sec.gov/Archives/edgar/data/1655210/000162828019005740/beyondmeat424b4.htm

108. Nathan Owens, 'Tyson plans own plant-based foods', *Arkansas Democrat Gazette*, 9 February 2019 https://www.arkansasonline.com/news/2019/feb/09/tyson-plans-own-plant-based-foods-20190/

109. Joel Crews, 'Tyson expands its plant-based brand to Europe', *Meat + Poultry*, 9 November 2020 https://www.meatpoultry.com/articles/24074-tyson-expands-its-plant-based-brand-to-europe; see also Sarah Min, 'Tyson, America's largest meat producer, sinks its teeth into fake meat', *CBS News*, 13 June 2019 https://www.cbsnews.com/news/tyson-vegan-meat-americas-largest-meat-producer-is-tearing-into-fake-meat/

110. Sam Chambers, 'Tesco's Fresh Food Helps Retailer Surmount Cost Pressures', *Bloomberg*, 11 April 2018 https://www.bloomberg.com/news/articles/2018-04-11/tesco-profit-leaps-as-fresh-food-sales-drive-retailer-s-growth

111. Josie Le Blond, 'World's first no-kill eggs go on sale in Berlin', the *Guardian*, 22 December 2018 https://www.theguardian.com/environment/2018/dec/22/worlds-first-no-kill-eggs-go-on-sale-in-berlin

112. Peter Allen, 'France and Germany to ban controversial practice of slaughtering male chicks in 2021', the *Telegraph*, 28 January 2020 https://www.telegraph.co.uk/news/2020/01/28/france-ban-controversial-practice-slaughtering-male-chicks-2021/ (Although we understand that Germany has been trying to enact this ban for some time, but it has been postponed many times.)

113. Massachusetts Minimum Size Requirements for Farm Animal Containment, Question 3 (2016) https://ballotpedia.org/Massachusetts_Minimum_Size_Requirements_for_Farm_Animal_Containment,_Question_3_(2016)#cite_note-products-11

114. Richie Davis, 'Cruel reality? Diemand Farm only one in Question 3 crosshairs', *Greenfield Recorder*, 14 October 2016 https://www.recorder.com/Diemand-Farm-future-tied-to-Question-3-5024360

115. Dan Charles, 'Most U.S. Egg Producers Are Now Choosing Cage-Free Houses', *The Salt*, National Public Radio, 15 January 2016 https://www.npr.org/sections/thesalt/2016/

01/15/463190984/most-new-hen-houses-are-now-cage-free; see also Jennifer Hashley and William A. Masters, 'Keeping Eggs Affordable: The Case Against Massachusetts Ballot Question 3', WBUR radio, 19 October 2016 https://www.wbur.org/cognoscenti/2016/10/19/the-case-against-massachusetts-ballot-question-3-farm-animal-welfare-william-a-masters-jennifer-hashley

116. Hashley and Masters, 'Keeping Eggs Affordable'

117. Michael Greger M.D. FACLM, 'Eggs & Cholesterol: Patently False & Misleading Claims', *Nutrition Facts.org*, 3 July 2013, Volume 13 https://nutritionfacts.org/video/eggs-and-cholesterol-patently-false-and-misleading-claims/

118. Elise Golan, Hayden Stewart, Fred Kuchler and Diansheng Dong, 'Can Low-Income Americans Afford a Healthy Diet?' United States Department of Agriculture, Economic Research Service, 1 November 2008 https://www.ers.usda.gov/amber-waves/2008/november/can-low-income-americans-afford-a-healthy-diet/; see also Jessie A. Satia, PhD, MPH, 'Diet-related disparities: Understanding the problem and accelerating solutions', *Journal of the Academy of Nutrition and Dietetics*, December 2009 https://www.ncbi.nlm.nih.gov/pmc/articles/PMC2729116/

119. Joshua Miller, 'Mass. ballot question could raise the price of eggs', *Boston Globe*, 7 January 2016 https://www.bostonglobe.com/metro/2016/01/07/mass-ballot-question-could-raise-price-eggs/2ekY9MwuE2dUpzXa8Kmt2H/story.html

120. 'Mass. ballot push would mandate cage-free eggs', reprinted from *Boston Globe* on *Yes on 3* website http://www.citizensfor farmanimals.com/media/mass-ballot-push-would-mandate-cage-free-eggs

121. 'Should Massachusetts require cage- and crate-free egg and meat products'. *Boston Globe*, 1 April 2016 https://www.bostonglobe.com/metro/regionals/north/2016/04/01/should-massachusetts-require-cage-and-crate-free-egg-and-meat-products/ayuu C7S3icYQWJpLxehySN/story.html

122. Christian M. Wade, 'State could again alter rules on chicken cages', *Salem News*, 3 October 2019 https://www.salemnews.com/news/local_news/state-could-again-alter-rules-on-chicken-cages/article_10ff4827-c68f-55b4-a053-42995a8ab6ab.html

123. Massachusetts Minimum Size Requirements for Farm Animal Containment, Question 3 (2016) https://ballotpedia.org/Massachusetts_Minimum_Size_Requirements_for_Farm_Animal_Containment,_Question_3_(2016)#Opposition_in-kind_donations

124. Wayne Pacelle, 'Massachusetts voters push farm animal measure to the ballot, with broad, powerful coalition', *Humane Society blog*, 28 June 2016 https://blog.humanesociety.org/2016/06/massachusetts-pushes-farm-animal-confinement-measure-to-ballot.html

125. Ballot Questions Committee Reports https://www.ocpf.us/Reports/BallotQuestionReports

126. For an enlightening analysis of the broader implications of this, see Gary Francione, *Rain Without Thunder: The Ideology of the Animal Rights Movement*, Temple University Press, Philadelphia, 1996

127. Office of the Los Angeles City Clerk, Vote Details http://cityclerk.lacity.org/cvvs/search/votedetails.cfm?voteid=100170&rnd=0.679474695793; Office of the Los Angeles City Clerk, Motion to Amend and Request http://clkrep.lacity.org/onlinedocs/2018/18-0538_mot_09-18-18.pdf; Office of the Los Angeles City Clerk, Personnel and Animal Welfare Committee Report http://clkrep.lacity.org/onlinedocs/2018/18-0538_rpt_paw_8-15-18.pdf

128. Sections 2023 and 3039 of the State of California's Fish and Game Code https://leginfo.legislature.ca.gov/faces/billTextClient.xhtml?bill_id=201920200AB44

129. Elaine S. Povich, 'Fur Clothing Bans Advance in More Cities and States', *Pew*, 5 September 2019 https://www.pewtrusts.org/en/research-and-analysis/blogs/stateline/2019/09/05/fur-clothing-bans-advance-in-more-cities-and-states; see also Maria LaMagna, 'San Francisco bans sale of fur, but Americans can't get enough of it', *Fur Commission USA*, 22 March 2018 https://furcommission.com/san-francisco-bans-sale-of-fur-but-americans-cant-get-enough-of-it/

130. After a public outcry, House of Fraser removed the items of fur they were selling, but there's nothing stopping them from selling fur items at another time. See Ben Chapman, 'Mike Ashley's House of Fraser removes fur products after customer backlash', the *Independent*, 22 November 2019 https://www.

independent.co.uk/news/business/news/house-of-fraser-removes-fur-mike-ashley-a9214421.html

131. Section 2023 of the State of California's Fish and Game Code https://leginfo.legislature.ca.gov/faces/billTextClient.xhtml?-bill_id=201920200AB44

132. 'Unknown but likely minor potential revenue losses: Potential decreased revenue, likely less than a few thousand dollars, to the FGPF due to potential decreases in recreational trapping license fee revenue and the elimination of fur dealer and fur agent licenses. Unknown but likely minor losses in state sales tax revenue to the General Fund.' Senate Rules Committee, Senate Floor Analyses, Bill Number AB 44, 9 September 2019 https://leginfo.legislature.ca.gov/faces/billAnalysisClient.xhtml?bill_id=201920200AB44

133. Video of Paul Koretz on the Los Angeles fur ban https://www.instagram.com/p/Bmm-9HZgQ-4/?utm_source=ig_twitter_share&igshid=fbviboc16yco

134. Hilary Hanson, 'Florence Kills An Estimated 5,500 Pigs, 3.4 Million Chickens And Turkeys In North Carolina', *Huffington Post*, 19 September 2018 https://www.huffingtonpost.co.uk/entry/pigs-chickens-killed-hurricane-florence_us_5ba15035e4b046313fc0213f?guccounter=1

135. Alan Herscovici, 'Anti-Fur Protesters Now Rebels Without A Cause?', *Truth About Fur*, 13 November 2017 https://www.truthaboutfur.com/blog/anti-fur-protesters-now-rebels-without-cause/

Chapter 5

1. Position of the Academy of Nutrition and Dietetics (formerly known as the American Dietetic Association): vegetarian diets https://www.ncbi.nlm.nih.gov/pubmed/19562864?fbclid=IwAR2oJ82_7brLHWAx8dRY5ZuPhUVJFBUVvmh4ymo6V-V5koDbhiqhfWxD3Oo

2. The Association of UK Dietitians https://www.bda.uk.com/food-health/food-facts.html

3. Dietitians Association of Australia, 'Vegan diets: everything you need to know' https://daa.asn.au/smart-eating-for-you/smart-eating-fast-facts/healthy-eating/vegan-diets-facts-tips-and-considerations/?fbclid=IwARoU72zdcF4tMvWFRDMNCwNLzmToauVJroVmLYiNpeJ1y3OczbnMoENdiog

4. Dietitians of Canada, 'What You Need to Know About Following a Vegan Eating Plan' http://www.unlockfood.ca/en/Articles/Vegetarian-and-Vegan-Diets/What-You-Need-to-Know-About-Following-a-Vegan-Eati.aspx?fbclid=IwAR2sioUYxyqYHJGk1pEEBqbtomLOZRgmkwRtpitCki5PoWZw-DhDhbX78Vg

5. Cleveland Clinic, 'Plant-based nutrition' https://my.clevelandclinic.org/health/articles/17593-understanding-vegetarianism-heart-health?fbclid=IwAR30JEc1JpTvIOmEoHN0D51uODoofDeNuivEG8fFGd3DcgobLvsYbjOqibM

6. Harvard Women's Health Watch, 'Becoming a vegetarian', Harvard Health Publishing, Harvard Medical School https://www.health.harvard.edu/staying-healthy/becoming-a-vegetarian?fbclid=IwAR3FnLhhh3YL26YogOsz8QvPvBY4FdoYscSpk1p8zT5Lgc8ZwZ1ZXBS4zys

7. Mayo Clinic, 'Vegetarian diet: How to get the best nutrition' https://www.mayoclinic.org/healthy-lifestyle/nutrition-and-healthy-eating/in-depth/vegetarian-diet/art-20046446?fbclid=IwAR0C-AZHH3hgDjqTrp2_AFdjSTe_UVCRk5a1FK9HE5dYwJ7gsJ44yHCKEjo

8. National Health Service, 'The vegan diet' https://www.nhs.uk/live-well/eat-well/the-vegan-diet/

9. Michael Greger M.D. FACLM, 'Uprooting the Leading Causes of Death', *Nutrition Facts.org*, 26 July 2012 https://nutritionfacts.org/video/uprooting-the-leading-causes-of-death/?fbclid=IwAR3Op-zp2n6RMNRv3nzZhMI6oU_NnidyqFSLqCLmRI7F5MMr386lAQTgatU

10. Morgan E. Levine, Jorge A. Suarez, Sebastian Brandhorst, Pinchas Cohen, Eileen M. Crimmins and Valter D. Longo, "Low Protein Intake Is Associated with a Major Reduction in IGF-1, Cancer, and Overall Mortality in the 65 and Younger but Not Older Population", *Cell Metabolism*, Vol. 19, No 3, 4 March 2014 http://www.cell.com/cell-metabolism/fulltext/S1550-4131(14)00062-X

11. American Heart Association, 'Vegetarian, Vegan and Meals Without Meat', 27 January 2017 http://www.heart.org/HEARTORG/HealthyLiving/HealthyEating/Vegetarian-Diets_UCM_306032_Article.jsp

12. In particular, carmine or E120 is made from the female cochineal insect https://en.wikipedia.org/wiki/Carmine

13. Natco chickpeas, https://www.tesco.com/groceries/en-GB/products/254869320; Natco green lentils, https://www.tesco.com/groceries/en-GB/products/287651164; see also Diane Vukovic, 'Cost of Vegan Protein vs. Animal Protein', *Plentous Veg*, 15 October 2014 http://plenteousveg.com/cost-vegan-protein-vs-animal-protein/

14. Creamfields 10 cheese slices 170g £.50, https://www.tesco.com/groceries/en-GB/products/299668011; Tesco Free From Coconut Oil Alternative To Chili Cheese Slices 180g £2.25, https://www.tesco.com/groceries/en-GB/products/306493304

15. Tesco double Gloucester chive and onion cheese slices 150g £1.90, https://www.tesco.com/groceries/en-GB/products/2997 69905

16. Tesco ripened French brie 190g £1.90, https://www.tesco.com/groceries/en-GB/products/259201095; Honestly Tasty shamembert 160g £8.00, https://honestlytasty.co.uk/collections/our-cheese/products/shamembert; Vacherin Mont D'Or 400g £14.95, https://www.finefoodspecialist.co.uk/vacherin-mont-d-or-500g?gclid=CjoKCQiA48j9BRC-ARIsAMQu3WT1_I_vPBTdzyzpctkfRnV3PmxPF5D2j_HWigF-mW_0kHAXS7 TnREsaAhdjEALw_wcB.

17. Woodside Farms 12 pork sausages 681g £1.20, https://www.tesco.com/groceries/en-GB/products/301801750; Tesco Plant Chef 6 herby bangers sausages 300g £1.75, https://www.tesco.com/groceries/en-GB/products/305044988

18. Jolly Hog 12 British chipolatas gluten free sausages 340g £8.16, https://www.tesco.com/groceries/en-GB/products/305965670; Beyond sausages 2 pack 200g £5.00, https://www.tesco.com/groceries/en-GB/products/304794239; Farminson & Co traditional saveloy 4 sausages 320g £7.95, https://www.farmison.com/our-meat/sausage/f-co-traditional-saveloy; Tesco organic fillet steak 190g £6.76, https://www.tesco.com/groceries/en-GB/products/252506460

19. Eat Vegan on $4 a Day Facebook page https://www.facebook.com/EatVeganOn4DollarsADay/

20. Molly Thompson, 'What Are the Variable and Fixed Costs in a Restaurant Operation?', *Chron* http://smallbusiness.chron.com/variable-fixed-costs-restaurant-operation-81771.html

21. Rosie Conroy, 'Our ultimate list of the 16 best burgers in London', *Squaremeal*, updated 24 August 2020 https://www.

squaremeal.co.uk/restaurants/best-for/best-burgers-in-london_1681

22. Website for Evolution Fast Food http://evolutionfastfood.com/

23. GlobalData Consumer, 'McDonalds and Nando's to launch vegan burgers in the UK', *Food Service*, 28 October 2020 https://www.verdictfoodservice.com/comment/vegan-mcdonalds-nandos/

24. Honestly Tasty Shamembert 160g £8, https://honestlytasty.co.uk/collections/our-cheese; see also Mouse's Favourite camembert 140g £8.99, https://www.thevegankindsupermarket.com/p/mouses-favourite-camembert-artisan-vegan-style-cheese-140g

25. Running even the simplest of searches, such as 'is vegan food more expensive', 'guide to low cost vegan' or 'vegan on a budget uk' will yield thousands of results in a few seconds on any web browser.

26. Centers for Disease Control, 'Zoonotic Diseases' https://www.cdc.gov/onehealth/basics/zoonotic-diseases.html

27. Jared Diamond, *Guns, Germs and Steel: a short history of everybody for the last 13,000 years*, Vintage Books, London, 2005, p. 207; see also Viveca Morris 'Op-Ed: COVID-19 shows that what we're doing to animals is killing us, too', *Los Angeles Times*, 2 April 2020 https://www.latimes.com/opinion/story/2020-04-02/coronavirus-pandemics-animals-habitat-ecology

28. Rob Wallace, *Big Farms Make Big Flu*, Monthly Review Press, New York, 2016, p. 251.

29. Jessica M Pearce-Duvet, 'The origin of human pathogens: evaluating the role of agriculture and domestic animals in the evolution of human disease', *Biological Reviews of the Cambridge Philosophical Society*, 81(3): 369-82, 4 May 2006, https://europepmc.org/article/med/16672105; see also Nathan D. Wolfe, Claire Panosian Dunavan and Jared Diamond, 'Origins of major human infectious diseases', *Nature*, 17 May 2007, 447, pp. 279–283 https://www.nature.com/articles/nature05775

30. See, for example, 'Measles', World Health Organization https://www.who.int/news-room/fact-sheets/detail/measles

31. 'Deforestation [resulting from mining and other extractive activities] . . . turned bushmeat from a subsistence food item into a commodity that supported logging camps in the thousands,

and, later, farming towns growing on the edges of the contracting forest.' Wallace, *Big Flu*, pp. 283

32. In July 2020, the UN Environment Program published a report entitled 'Preventing the next pandemic – Zoonotic diseases and how to break the chain of transmission' where they identified 'seven major anthropogenic drivers of zoonotic disease emergence', including increasing demand for animal protein, more intensive and unsustainable farming practices, increased use and exploitation of wildlife, global travel facilitating spread of diseases and the climate crisis. https://www.unenvironment.org/resources/report/preventing-future-zoonotic-disease-outbreaks-protecting-environment-animals-and

33. For an overview on the contribution by animal agriculture to antibiotics resistance, see 'Antimicrobial resistance in the food chain', World Health Organization, November 2017 https://www.who.int/foodsafety/areas_work/antimicrobial-resistance/amrfoodchain/en/

34. Wallace, *Big Flu*, p. 305

Chapter 6

1. *Livestock's Long Shadow*, Food and Agriculture Organization of the United Nations, 2006 http://www.fao.org/3/a0701e/a0701e00.htm

2. Robert Goodland and Jeff Anhang, *Livestock and Climate Change: What if the key actors in climate change are... cows, pigs and chickens?*, WorldWatch Institute, November/December 2009 http://templatelab.com/livestock-and-climate-change/ http://www.worldwatch.org/node/6294

3. Robert Goodland and Jeff Anhang, 'Response to "Livestock and greenhouse gas emissions: The importance of getting the numbers right," by Herrero et al', *A Well-Fed World*, https://awfw.org/wp-content/uploads/pdf/Goodland-Anhang-Livestock-GHG-1-7-12.pdf; see also Robert Goodland, '"Livestock and Climate Change": Critical Comments and Responses', *World Watch*, Vol 23, No. 2, March/April 2010 https://web.archive.orgweb/20110818173158/http://awellfedworld.org/sites/awellfedworld.org/files/pdf/WWMLivestock-ClimateResponses.pdf; see also other resources appearing on their website http://www.chompingclimatechange.org/publications/articles/

4. Martin Hickman, 'Study claims meat creates half of all greenhouse gases', *Independent*, 1 November 2019 https://www.independent.co.uk/environment/climate-change/study-claims-meat-creates-half-of-all-greenhouse-gases-1812909.html; see also Vance Lehmkuhl, 'Livestock and climate: Whose numbers are more credible?', *The Philadelphia Inquirer*, 2 March 2012 https://www.inquirer.com/philly/blogs/earth-to-philly/Livestock-and-climate-Whose-numbers-are-more-credible.html

5. Food and Agriculture Organization of the United Nations, *Tackling Climate Change through Livestock: A global assessment of emissions and mitigation opportunities*, Rome, 2013 http://www.fao.org/3/i3437e/i3437e00.htm

6. *Ibid.*

7. Brent Kim, Roni Neff, Raychel Santo, and Juliana Vigorito, *The Importance of Reducing Animal Product Consumption and Wasted Food in Mitigating Catastrophic Climate Change*, Johns Hopkins Center for a Liveable Future, 1 December 2015 https://clf.jhsph.edu/publications/importance-reducing-animal-product-consumption-and-wasted-food-mitigating-catastrophic

8. Springmann, Marco & Clark, Michael & Mason-D'Croz, Daniel & Wiebe, Keith & Bodirsky, Benjamin & Lassaletta, Luis & Vries, Wim & Vermeulen, Sonja & Herrero, Mario & Carlson, Kimberly & Jonell, Malin & Troell, Max & Declerck, Fabrice & Gordon, Line & Zurayk, Rami & Scarborough, Peter & Rayner, Mike & Loken, Brent & Fanzo, Jess & Willett, Walter, 'Options for keeping the food system within environmental limits', *Nature*, 2018 https://www.researchgate.net/publication/328200342_Options_for_keeping_the_food_system_within_environmental_limits

9. J. Poore and T. Nemecek, 'Reducing food's environmental impacts through producers and consumers', *Science*, 1 June 2018 and 22 February 2019 (erratum) https://science.sciencemag.org/content/360/6392/987

10. 'Food in the Anthropocene: the EAT–*Lancet* Commission on healthy diets from sustainable food systems', *The Lancet*, 16 January 2019 https://www.thelancet.com/commissions/EAT; and 'The Global Syndemic of Obesity, Undernutrition, and Climate Change: The Lancet Commission report', *The Lancet*, 16 January 2019 https://www.thelancet.com/commissions/global-syndemic

11. Jeff McMahon, 'Meat And Agriculture Are Worse For The Climate Than Power Generation, Steven Chu Says', *Forbes*, 4 April 2019 https://www.forbes.com/sites/jeffmcmahon/2019/04/04/meat-and-agriculture-are-worse-for-the-climate-than-dirty-energy-steven-chu-says/?fbclid=IwAR3VwYg7MM1rHQDfnah_xOGKqjDcH-9y30GSnXEWYUJP9uVzWoPhcyj-4xQ#5f6130a911f9

12. Robert Goodland and Jeff Anhang, 'Response to "Livestock and greenhouse gas emissions: The importance of getting the numbers right," by Herrero et al', A Well-Fed World https://awfw.org/wp-content/uploads/pdf/Goodland-Anhang-Livestock-GHG-1-7-12.pdf

13. Christian J. Peters, Jamie Picardy, Amelia F. Darrouzet-Nardi, Jennifer L. Wilkins, Timothy S. Griffin, Gary W. Fick, 'Carrying capacity of U.S. agricultural land: Ten diet scenarios', *Elementa Science of the Anthropocene*, 2016 https://online.ucpress.edu/elementa/article/doi/10.12952/journal.elementa.000116/112904/Carrying-capacity-of-U-S-agricultural-land-Ten

14. Springmann et al, 'Options for keeping the food system within environmental limits'

15. Food and Agriculture Organization of the United Nations, 'FAO's role in animal production' http://www.fao.org/animal-production/en/

16. Food and Agriculture Organization of the United Nations, 'Livestock on Grazing Lands' http://www.fao.org/3/x5304e/x5304e03.htm

17. Current World Population https://www.worldometers.info/world-population/

18. FAO, 'Livestock on Grazing Lands'

19. See Christian Parenti, *Tropic of Chaos: Climate Change and the New Geography of Violence*. Nation Books, New York, 2011.

Chapter 8

1. Angela Davis In Conversation at WOW Global 24, June 2020 https://www.youtube.com/watch?v=-kJlHwU1zmg]

Index

Unbound is the world's first crowdfunding publisher, established in 2011.

We believe that wonderful things can happen when you clear a path for people who share a passion. That's why we've built a platform that brings together readers and authors to crowdfund books they believe in – and give fresh ideas that don't fit the traditional mould the chance they deserve.

This book is in your hands because readers made it possible. Everyone who pledged their support is listed below. Join them by visiting unbound.com and supporting a book today.

A.U.S.

Heba Abuabdou

Keith Adsley

Imogen Allred

Raffaella Alto

Tobias Alvarsson

Tina Ambury

Mark Ames

T. D. Ankers

Cheryl Ashman

Jim Atherton

Ellie Atkins

Sally Austen

Meredith Avila-Camarena

Kirsty Baggs-Morgan

David Baillie

Florence Ballard

Michael Balletto

Helen Barker

Matthew Bate

Val Bayliss-Brideaux

Nick Bedi

Jaime Bell

Belle Afrique

Phillip Bennett-Richards

Harry Bolman

Barbara Bolton

Becky Bolton

Naomi Boxall

John Boyce

Petra Breunig

Rob Broder

Jenny Brown

Tomas Brown

Kelly Brozo

Nikala Bullard

John Bullwinkel

Sara Buscj

Clare Byrne

Laura Callan

Hillary Cannon

Robert Caperell

Tom Carr

Andrew Carroll

Rosemary Carroll

Dirk Cavens

Geertrui Cazaux

Jacqueline Chan

Matt Charalambides

Monique Charalambides

Charalambides Family

Dominique Cheshire

Alex Ciccone

Stephany Clark

Ella Clarke

Lynsey Clayton - Monsoon
   of Random

Emma Clifford

Caryn Cohen

Elizabeth Collins

Ian Convery

Harry Cooke

Leanne Cooper

Mark Cooper

Angela Corcoran

Alex Counts

Chris Coupland

Elyse Crawford

Wayne Crawford

Mary R. Crumpton

Michelle Cuninghame

Jennifer Cwiok

Becky Dahl

Paul Daly

Evan Danziger

Geoffrey Darnton

Viran Daya

Foppe de Haan

Melissa De Santis

Hal Dean

Lauren Dean

Danny DeMarco

Claire Desroches

MacKenzie DeVito

Ruchi Dhir

Deanna Di Biasio

John Dolan

Lisa Dollinger

Kevin Donnellon

Kip Dorrell

Tracy Douglas-Keegan

Stella Downes

Michail Dim.
    Drakomathioulakis

Alan Driver

Erica Edwards

Michael Elliott

David Eppish

Ruth Ersapah

Hayal Ersöz

Robert Espin

European Citizen

Nade Evans

Yara Evans

Mike Farragher

Brendan Farrelly

Serena Fazzolari

Samantha Feeney

Emily Sigala Flagstad

Lisa Forbes

Laura Fortune

Isa Fowler

Michele Fox

Tamas Frajka

Bridget Frost

Yui Fujiyama

Caitlin Galer-Unti

Aggie Gallagher

Steven Gallagher

Dana Genito

Olivia Genito

Citlali Gerits

Erin Gianferrara

Gianluca, Leela, Ayni and
    Alya

Kathleen Gibbons Blasko

Emanuele Giorgione

Rob Glassford

GMarkC

Lyndsey Goddard

Inácio Gómez

Anthony Goodesmith

Jakub Grabowski

Francesca Greco

David Green

Phoebe Greenough
    Guerreiro

Shardae Grenfell

Jacqueline Guerin

Jeremy Hancock

Hanan Harchol

Sue Harries

Alinta Hawkins

Sarah Hayton

Sue Hecht

Samuel Hedley

Michaela Hennemann

Peter Hewitt

Sandra Higgins

Melissa Hilfers

Ben Hinceman

Loen Hoang

Peter Hobbins

Denise Hof

John and Cornelia Holton

Angela Hughes-Beddome

Rowena Humphreys

I Just Wanted

Mex Ibrahim

Indy

Frank Ip

Johanna Irving

Kara Irwin

Sharon Jakobowitz

Nivi Jasa

Austra Jenner-Parson

Mark Jenner-Parson

Lynda Joeman

Jack Johnson

Andres Kabel

Emmie Kakkas

Helen Kamenjuk

Amy Kean, The Girl Who
    Gave Zero Fucks

Barry Kelleher

Soniya Kenth

Jymit Khondhu

Dan Kieran

Justina Kolberg

Lena Kolbowski

K. Kolshus

D. I. Kovacic

Patrick Kowalczyj

Michele Krauss

Kristina Kyser

Arthur & Sheila Lampert

Lori Lampert

Samantha Lampert

Alexandra Leader

Robyn Lee

The Leese Family

Scott Leger

Carol Leister

David Leister

Anastasia Lewis

Bonnie Lewis

Angela Li

Libby & Dorito

Valter Liblik

Charlotte Lincoln and
    Matthew Crisp

Melissa Liu Frey

Alexandra Logue

Jacqueline Lopez

Loucas Loucaides

Katharine Loucaidou

Jo MacArthur

Benjamin S. MacEllen

Tomi Makanjuola

Catherine Makin

Emilie Mancini

Shayna Mandel

Ivano Mannella

Keith Mantell

Matthew Maran

Judith Marr

Ambra Marras

Helen Martin-Wright

Sidney Marton

Joshua May

Tabitha Mayall

Rosalind and Clayton
  McCallard

Hollis McCartney

Damon McDonald

Siobhán McGrath

Carole McIntosh

Andrew Meade

Dee Mehta

Davide Melia

Giovanni Menniti

Clare Minchington

Lynette Gudicello Ming

John Mitchinson

Napak Molyneux

Justin P. Moore

Jeff Moss

Elaine Mulingani

Ruth Mumma

Pat Murphy

Cressida Murray

Dirk Myers

Carlo Navato

Marika Netzel

Lauren Nkuranga

Helen Norton

Kevin O'Keeffe

Barbara Oppo

Emma Osborne

Nuri Özlü

Zile Ozols

Julie Palmer-Hoffman

Louise Palmer-Masterton

Aasiya PanchbhAya

Jennifer Pardoe

Pierre Parent

Daniel Parisi

Brian Patton

Rosie Pearson

Laurence Peberdy

Patricia Petrat

Antoine Plantoine

Michael Pollak

Justin Pollard

Chiara Polti

Marlaine Pretorius

Kelly Price

Annayah Prosser

Sareta Puri

Molly Puttnam

Jill Regan

Hillary Rettig

Ina Richter

Silvia Rietdijk

Frances Robinson

Peter Rogers

Rogue Vegan

Cyndi Rook

Katia Rossi

Zoe Rozansky

Dayna Rozental

Chiara Saitta

Martin Salway

Marian Savill

Shannon Schnibbe

Dale & Allie Schultz

Moko Sellars

Bani Sethi

Laurence Shapiro

Kadri Sikk

Anna Simonelli

Pasquale Simonelli

Silvia Siret

Michael Sisk

Geoffry Smalley

Andrew Smith

Louise Smith

Maria Solberg Williams

Rebecca Sopp

Cari Spivack

Wendy Staden

Clair Stanway

Ellie Stanway

Lucy Stewart

Louise Strom

Cathy Swift

Shane Tarrant

Lucy Teagle

Robin Tedlock

George Theodosiou

Kelly Theodosiou

Tim Theodosiou

Louie Thomas

Helen Thompson

Seth Tibbott

Martin Treanor

Alex Turner

James Turner

Rachel Ulanet

Gabriel Uriarte

Francesca Valluzzi

Emily Van Engel

Christopher Vaughn

The Vegan Ronin

Laveen Venugopalan

Ireene Viktor

Cristiano Vitelli

Mallory Warren

Peggy Warren

Kevin Watkinson

Velest Way

Marika Weinhardt and
    Thomas Ottey

Hayley Wells

Sarah Whiddett

Chris White

Deborah Wicks

Paige Wilkie

Anni Williams

Stephanie Williams

Ashley Wilson

Paul Wren

Jason Yalen

Claire Yip

James Young

Sonia Zaame